Twayne's United States Authors Series

EDITOR OF THIS VOLUME

Warren French

Indiana University

Joyce Carol Oates

TUSAS 321

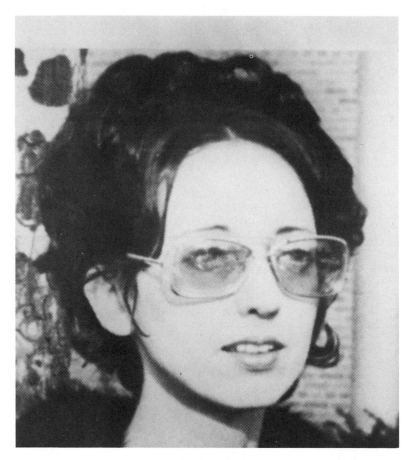

Joyce Carol Oates

JOYCE CAROL OATES

By JOANNE V. CREIGHTON

Wayne State University

TWAYNE PUBLISHERS
A DIVISION OF G. K. HALL & CO., BOSTON

813
O//zc

Library of Congress Cataloging in Publication Data

Creighton, Joanne V   1942-
Joyce Carol Oates.

(Twayne's United States authors series ; TUSAS 321)
Bibliography: p. 161-69
Includes index.
1. Oates, Joyce Carol, 1938-   —Criticism and
interpretation. I. French, Warren G., 1922-
PS3565.A8Z6   813'.5'4   78-27318
ISBN 0-8057-7212-X

∠W
2oo338

To my son, William

Contents

About the Author

Completing a bachelor's degree in English from the University of Wisconsin in 1964, a master's from Harvard University in 1965, and a doctorate from the University of Michigan in 1969, Joanne V. Creighton has since 1968 taught at Wayne State University where she is now an Associate Professor of English. Before undertaking this study, her research interests centered largely on the work of William Faulkner, focusing particularly on his reworking of earlier short stories into longer works. This research project resulted in several articles and a book, *William Faulkner's Craft of Revision* (1977).

Her interest in Joyce Carol Oates is linked in part to the affinities in Oates's early work with Faulkner's, but also to a number of other probable causes, such as the way her own background, experiences, and environments have in many ways paralleled Oates's; her puzzlement over the effect Oates's work has had upon readers; her feeling that Oates's fiction has been imperfectly recognized and explicated. She has read papers on Oates at the MLA convention and at the annual meeting of the Michigan Academy of Science, Arts, and Letters and has published two articles, "Unliberated Women in Joyce Carol Oates's Fiction," *World Literature Written in English*, 17 (April 1978), 165-75, and "Joyce Carol Oates's Craftsmanship in *The Wheel of Love*," *Studies in Short Fiction*, 15 (Fall 1978), which have been revised and incorporated into this study, thanks to the kind permission of the editors of these journals.

Preface

Joyce Carol Oates is one of the more widely known and generally misunderstood of contemporary writers. The sheer quantity of her work, coupled as it is with her relatively young age, has made her something of a cultural phenomenon: by 1977 at age thirty-nine, she had published eight novels, ten collections of short stories, six collections of poems, two books of criticism, a play, a novella, and a prodigious bulk of uncollected material. Although her books are often popular with a segment of the reading public and are sometimes favorably reviewed, they have received relatively little serious study by literary critics. Yet she certainly has produced a canon of sufficiently impressive quantity, range, depth, and complexity to merit more extensive critical attention now in the midstream of her career. I hope that this study will offer perspectives on her unique and continuing contribution to American fiction. Because of the bulk of Oates's writing, I have limited the scope of this book to those volumes of fiction—short stories and novels—published from 1963–1976. Poetry, drama, and uncollected fiction are excluded, and it may be that all the works included here will ultimately be seen as part of Oates's "apprenticeship," since no abatement in her productivity is evident.

In Chapter One, I attempt to place Oates within appropriate biographical and critical contexts. An important critic in her own right who argues that an artist does not create in isolation but draws from and synthesizes the communal consciousness of his culture, Oates sets forth a consistent critical theory. She claims that her own fiction presents for the reader's persual hypothetical propositions about human personality; one of the objectives of this study is to examine critically these hypotheses. In Chapter Two, I consider the first three published volumes as Oates's apprenticeship. In the two collections of short stories, *By the North Gate* and *Upon the Sweeping Flood*, in particular, Oates skillfully evokes the back-country world of her fictitious and symbolic Eden County. They, along with her first novel, *With Shuddering Fall*, establish the themes, structural patterns, and character types which will dominate her fiction for the next several years. In Chapter Three, I look at the next three novels, *A Garden of Earthly Delights, Expensive People,* and *them,* which form a trilogy focusing on groups in American society—migrant workers, affluent suburbanites, and urban poor. Each novel depicts the quest of the central male character to achieve liberation from constricting sociological and psychological forces. In Chapter Four I study the next two novels, *Wonderland* and *Do With Me What You Will,* in which educated professionals search for selfhood amid increasingly abstract notions of personality derived from medicine and law. In Chapter Five I examine Oates's most ambitious novels, *The Assassins* and *Childwold,* in which she presents the characters both as individuals and as disharmonious fragments of a larger Self. In Chapter Six I peruse several of Oates's short-story collections seeking to isolate her characteristic style and themes and to show the range of her technical experimentation.

Just as Joyce Carol Oates's works are in the forms of hypothetical explorations of the nature of experience, so too is my explication of them in the chapters to follow a hypothetical statement, one which I hope will help to stimulate the participatory readership which Oates desires for her work, and deserves. It seems to me that now, in the midstream of her career, Oates stands in a rather anomalous position in relationship to an audience. Perhaps in part because some of her works have sold well with a popular audience, and because of her extraordinary productivity and reputation as an indifferent stylist, and because of the often shocking and unrelenting violence, madness, and emotional distress that she chronicles, Joyce Carol Oates has been categorized and dismissed as a "popular" writer by much of the academic and intellectual community. Yet Oates is one of the most serious and intellectual of contemporary writers, whose distinctive blend of compelling, hallucinatory realism with "complex propositions about the nature of personality" places great demands on the reader. In the final chapter of this study I will examine more closely the nature of those demands and attempt to evaluate her work from a reader-response perspective, assessing the strengths and limitations of this prolific writer, whose talent and dedication to her craft could make her one of the most significant writers of our era.

July 1978

Acknowledgments

I wish to express my thanks to Black Sparrow Press for permission to quote from *The Hungry Ghosts,* to Vanguard Press for permission to quote from Oates's other works, and to Dale Boesky for permission to quote from his published letters from Oates. I have profited immensely from the conversations, critical readings of portions of my manuscript, and encouragement of various friends and colleagues, especially from my sister Dr. Judith V. May, as well as Doctors Henry Golemba, Gladys Leithauser, Ruth and John Reed, Harry Smallenburg, and Paul Sporn, and from the highly stimulating class discussions and essays of my students at Wayne State University in English 370—Joyce Carol Oates—and English 774—American Women Fiction Writers. I thank Kathy Zamora for her professional typing and Warren French for his careful editing of the text. Finally, I am especially grateful to Joyce Carol Oates herself, who has graciously responded both by mail and in person to my queries about her work and who has nurtured a friendship quite apart from our roles as author and critic. Of course, I am solely responsible for the views expressed in the text.

Chronology

1938   Born June 16, daughter of Caroline and Frederick Oates, eldest of three children. Grew up in the countryside of Erie County outside Lockport, New York, on maternal grandparents' farm.

1956–   Attended Syracuse University on New York State Regents
1960   scholarship. Phi Beta Kappa; class valedictorian; earned B.A. in English, minor in philosophy.

1959   Cowinner, first prize, *Mademoiselle* College Fiction Contest for "In the Old World."

1960–   Attended University of Wisconsin, Madison, on fellowship;
1961   1961, met and married Raymond Joseph Smith; earned M.A. in English.

1961–   Lived in Beaumont, Texas; started work on Ph.D. at Rice
1962   University, Houston.

1962–   Taught English at University of Detroit.
1967

1963   *By the North Gate* (stories).

1964   *With Shuddering Fall* (novel).

1965   "The Sweet Enemy" (play) premiered at Actor's Playhouse, New York City.

1966   *Upon the Sweeping Flood* (stories); National Endowment for the Humanities Grant.

1967–   Guggenheim Fellowship.
1968

1967   Joined Department of English, University of Windsor, Windsor, Ontario; *A Garden of Earthly Delights* (novel); first prize, O. Henry Prize Awards, for "In the Region of Ice."

1968   *Expensive People* (novel); *Women in Love* (poems); Richard and Hilda Rosenthal Foundation Award of the National Institute of Arts and Letters for *A Garden of Earthly Delights;* National Endowment for the Humanities Grant.

1969   *Anonymous Sins* (poems); *them* (novel); first prize, Emily

Clark Balch Short Story Competition, for "Convalescing"; second prize, O. Henry Prize Awards, for "Accomplished Desires."

1970 *Love and Its Derangements* (poems); *The Wheel of Love* (stories); "Sunday Dinner" (play) premiered at American Place Theatre, New York City; National Book Award for *them;* Special Award for continuing achievement, O. Henry Prize Awards.

1971– Lived in London, England.
1972

1971 *Wonderland* (novel).

1972 *The Edge of Impossibility* (essays); *Marriages and Infidelities* (stories); "Ontological Proof of My Existence" (play) premiered at Cubiculo Theatre, New York City; second prize, O. Henry Prize Awards for "Saul Bird Says: Relate! Communicate! Liberate!" (also entitled "Pilgrims' Progress").

1973 *Angel Fire* (poems); *Dreaming America* (poems); *Do With Me What You Will* (novel); "Miracle Play" (play) premiered at Playhouse II Theatre, New York City; first prize, O. Henry Prize Awards for "The Dead."

1974 *The Goddess and Other Women* (stories); *New Heaven, New Earth* (essays); *The Hungry Ghosts* (stories); *Miracle Play* (play); *Where Are You Going, Where Have You Been?* (stories).

1975 *The Assassins* (novel); *The Fabulous Beasts* (poems); *The Poisoned Kiss* (stories); *The Seduction* (stories); Lotus Club Award of Merit.

1976 *Crossing the Border* (stories); *The Triumph of the Spider Monkey* (novella); *Childwold* (novel).

1977 *Night-Side* (stories).

1978 *Women Whose Lives are Food, Men Whose Lives are Money* (poems); *The Son of the Morning* (forthcoming novel); *All the Good People I've Left Behind* (forthcoming stories); elected to the American Academy and Institute of Arts and Letters; attended Soviet-American Writers Conference, New York City.

1978– Writer-in-Residence, Princeton University.
1979

CHAPTER 1

The Myth of the Isolated Artist

I A Private Life

JOYCE Carol Oates claims that much of her fiction is personal, "but distorted a little, made into fiction. What excites me about writing is the uses I can make of myself, of various small adventures, errors, miscalculations, stunning discoveries, near-disasters, and occasional reversals of everything, but so worked into a fictional structure that no one could guess how autobiographical it all is."[1] Indeed, no one could. She lives what appears to be a quiet, serene life, cut off from the violence, brutality, and emotional duress which typifies her fiction. Oates also says that she likes to combine herself with another person to form a "third person, a 'fictional' person." She playfully warns her interviewer "that with the least provocation (a few hints of your personal life, let's say, your appearance, your house and setting), I could 'go into' your personality and try to imagine it, try to find a way of dramatizing it. I am fascinated by people I meet, or don't meet, people I only correspond with, or read about; and I hope my interest in them isn't vampiristic, because I don't want to take life from them, but only to honor the life in them, to give some permanent form to their personalities."[2] While Oates has transformed into fiction many of the people she has known, most of the places she has lived, and many of the news events—major and minor—of our time, her disarming modesty and graciousness keep private all but the baldest facts about her personal life.

She was born June 16, 1938, the eldest of three children of Caroline and Frederick Oates, and lived until she was seventeen in Erie County, outside of Lockport in western New York State, a locale that undoubtedly inspired the creation of Oates's own fictional Eden County, the setting of a number of her volumes. Similarly, her Catholic, working-class, rural origins give a sense of authenticity to the characterization in her early fiction. Although Oates has mentioned cryptically that "terrible things happened" during her childhood,[3] she does not go into detail. Furthermore, while emotionally charged familial relationships are at the heart of her fiction, she gives no clues about how much of her considerable insight into parent-child and sibling relationships is based on personal experience. With characteristic privacy, she makes only generous comments about her parents. For example, in one interview she mentions their innate artistic talent: her father, a tool-and-die designer, who had to quit school at about the seventh grade to go to work, has "always been able to play the violin and the piano—*instinctively*"; her mother is creative with flowers and the house: "if I have any artistic talent, I think I inherited it from them." She does point out the importance of her life in the country—on her maternal grandparents' farm—in shaping her character: "The real clue to me is that I'm like certain people who are not really understood—Jung and Heidegger are good examples—people of peasant stock, from the country, who then come into a world of literature and philosophy. Part of us is very intellectual, wanting to read all the books in the library—or even wanting to *write* all the books in the library. Then there's the other side of us, which is sheer silence, inarticulate—the silence of nature, of the sky, of pure being."[4]

Oates claims that as a child she was not exposed to much "art," but one book she did have which profoundly affected her was *Alice in Wonderland and Through the Looking-Glass*, an influence which one can trace imagistically in her fiction. More important, though, are the psychological implications of the text which she says have "worked their way into the very fiber of my being." She explains them as follows:

A child triumphs.—The Child in us, which may be called our instincts or intuitive powers, is always superior to the snarls of the rational mind, and if we have faith in it and attempt to establish a rapport with it, we will always triumph.

Salvation is assured. All the animals win: The pawn becomes a queen.— Whether through our own strenuous activity or through what used to be called "grace," we will transcend the present; our personalities are layers upon layers, moving toward a kind of completion.

"You're nothing but a pack of cards."—A profound recognition, the declaration of the Child when confronted with the enormous ego-centered complexities of the so-called adult world.

"It's a huge game of chess that's being played all over the world if this is the world at all, you know. Oh, what fun it is! How I *wish* I was one of them! . . ." Alice exclaims.—She is, once again, profoundly right. A novelist recognizes this truth every day: Though one can be detached from the activities of life, seeing them as no more than games, it is necessary to get down there in the game as well, to play it with as much enthusiasm as possible. Everyone is playing and no one is left out. The game is *being played* and we are participants, not really controlling the game, but fulfilling it in some existential, mysterious way. In any case, a victory of some kind is assured.[5]

The valuing of the instinctual and intuitive, the belief in the possibility of transcendence of the ego, and the need to be involved in the "game"—the existential reality of life—are truths which lie at the heart of her fiction. Equally important, however, are the nightmarish aspects of Carroll's world which are echoed in Oates's, especially in her novel *Wonderland.*

She attended a one-room schoolhouse where the education, she observes, was not particularly good. After junior high in Lockport, she took a bus to high school outside of Buffalo, where she was fortunate, she says, to receive a sound education. She isolates Henry David Thoreau's *Walden* and Fyodor Dostoevsky's *The Brothers Karamazov* as having "a powerful effect" on her at this time. It was at Syracuse University, which she entered at age seventeen, however, where the excitement of the world of books took tenacious hold of Joyce Carol Oates. Here she read William Faulkner, a significant influence on her writing, who she claimed "bowled" her over. "Then Kafka. . . . Later, Freud, Nietzsche, Mann—they're almost real personalities in my life. And Dostoevsky and Melville."[6] She became then and remains today a voracious reader of literature, philosophy, and psychology. "I like to write, but I really love to read: that must be the greatest pleasure of civilization."[7] A recipient of a New York State Regents' Scholarship and a Syracuse scholarship, she was an outstanding student, valedictorian of her 1960 class with a B.A. in English and a minor in philosophy. In fact, her creative-writing professor, Donald A. Dike, says quite unequivocally that "she was the most brilliant student we've ever had here." During her college years she won the first of her many awards, first prize in *Mademoiselle* magazine's college fiction contest for her story "In the Old World." Professor Dike, commenting amusingly upon her creative productivity, claims that while she wrote mostly stories, "about once a term she'd drop a 400-page novel on my desk."[8]

In 1960 Oates attended the University of Wisconsin in Madison, completing an M.A. in English in 1961. At a faculty tea she met fellow graduate student Raymond Smith, whom she married a short time later: "It was very romantic," Oates observes.[9] She moved with her husband to his first teaching job in Beaumont, Texas, and she commuted briefly to Rice University in Houston where she began a Ph.D. in English. But the story she tells about this experience is that while browsing in the library, quite by accident, she came across one of her stories in Martha Foley's *Best American Short Stories* and decided then to become a professional writer. In 1962 the Smiths moved to Detroit where Oates was employed as an English instructor at the University of Detroit, while her husband taught English at Wayne State University. She skillfully evokes the city of Detroit as a setting for many of her stories and two novels, *them* and *Do With Me What You Will*. A small Catholic university, similar to the University of Detroit, is the setting for some of her stories, most notably "The Dead."

In 1966 Raymond Smith took a position in the English Department at the University of Windsor in Ontario; the following year he was joined by his wife. Frequent courses taught by Mrs. Smith, as she is called there, include literature and psychology, modern world literature, and creative writing. She has commented often upon how much she enjoys the give-and-take of teaching and the academic environment itself. Her academic satires, many collected in *The Hungry Ghosts*, also attest to her awareness of the fears, phobias, and pretensions of that world. Moreover, her sensitivity to the tensions, rewards, and disappointments of the special relationship of teacher-student is evident in many of her works. The Smiths are landed immigrants in Canada who retain their American citizenship and do not consider themselves to be Canadian. So far, at least, Oates's work has been set in American experience; only her academic satires and a recent collection, *Crossing the Border*, take place in Canada, and they focus largely on Americans who have crossed the border.

Seemingly contented with the life she leads, Joyce Carol Oates does admit to one period of personal crisis, in 1971, when she felt bogged down with social commitments and close to collapse. But fortunately her husband took a sabbatical leave that year and while in London, England, for the year, she had a chance to rest and to work out her problem. She mentions that the story "Plot" was written out of that personal distress, and she sees it as a kind of triumphant demonstration of the ability of the artist to use art therapeutically. "I found a fabric of some kind to absorb the various emotions that were drawing me under."[10] "So I feel that literature is wonderfully optimistic, instructive, because it so often demonstrates how human beings get through things, maneuver themselves through chaos, and then *write about it.*"[11] That she was thirty-three at this time of crisis in her life she carefully notes, and adds that she believes that many people have such a turning point in their lives at approximately that age. Now she claims that she has restructured her life so that she no longer does anything she does not want to do. A large part of her contentment comes from a professed detachment from the "ego personality," a remark which is illuminated by a consideration of her public self, the Joyce Carol Oates who sees herself as a "voice" of the "communal consciousness" of our culture.[12]

II *A Visionary Perspective*

Joyce Carol Oates, a fine critic in her own right, has commented extensively upon the nature of art both in relationship to the works of specific writers and in general. In addition to her two books of critical essays, *The Edge of Impossibility: Tragic Forms in Literature* and *New Heaven, New Earth: The Visionary Experience in Literature*, Oates's letters, notes, essays, and reviews appear frequently in such diverse publications as *New York Times Book Review* and *Esquire, Journal of Aesthetics and Art Criticism* and *Writer, Philosophical Quarterly* and *Mademoiselle, Partisan Review* and *Psychology Today.* She has also responded thoughtfully, and sometimes lengthily, to interviewers' questions about her views and her craftsmanship. What emerges from her critical commentary is an articulated philosophical and aesthetic position which helps to explain what she is attempting to do in her fiction. The aesthetic and philosophy which underlie her criticism become theme and vision in her fiction.

Central to her thought is a visionary conception of human experience, the belief that a gradual transformation of Western culture is taking place, that "the collective mind of our world is making a supreme effort to transcend itself."[13] What is being transcended and must be transcended, in Oates's view, is the ego-consciousness of our culture. "The human ego," Oates claims, "has too long imagined itself the supreme form of consciousness in the universe."[14] One of the "holiest myths" of Western culture is "the unique, proud, isolated entity of a 'self.'"[15] Growing out of the I and not-I dualism that has dominated Western thought for centuries, this myth, Oates points out in *New Heaven, New Earth*, finds its roots in the Renaissance in the elevation of noble man over nature, its continuation in the Romantic period with the exaltation of the subjective consciousness, and its modern-day evolution in existentialism in which man creates himself out of his own consciousness in an indifferent, hostile, or absurd universe. Oates argues that Freudian psychology, which has shaped so much of modern thought, has perpetuated this myth in the dialectics of the id and the ego and the equation of mental health with the ego's dominion over the id: "Where Id is, there shall Ego be."[16]

Oates does not find that this dualism has been a deterrent to art; on the contrary, out of it has grown our great tragic tradition which she so admires and about which she has written so perceptively. Tragedy, Oates claims, grows out of a break between the self and the community, the individual's sense of isolation. It is the expression of a unique human being's attempt to create himself in his own image, his attempt to assert the primacy of the human ego. For Oates, the quintessential modern expression of the tragic myth is Thomas Mann's *Dr. Faustus*. Adrian Leverkühn is Mann's most exalted embodiment of the artist. In him he portrays an intellectuality so total that it can find no object beyond itself. In him man's will is triumphant.[17]

Similarly Oates claims that the "man who 'masters' every aspect of his own being, subduing or obliterating his own natural instincts, leaving nothing to be unknown, uninvestigated," has been "the ideal of our culture, whether he is an industrialist or a 'disinterested' scientist or a literary man." But now, however, Oates feels that diverse groups in our society, as well as many of the best poets and writers, are questioning this ideal, or reacting against it, or moving beyond it. She feels that our culture is going through a transition which she calls "the death throes of the Renaissance."[18] Some writers, who are reacting against the ideal of the conquering human intellect but who are still locked in an I/It duality, have swung to the opposite extreme. Presuming that man's intellect does not belong 'in nature,' they believe that great works of art should spring spontaneously out of the unconscious, as if only the primitive 'id' were truly natural. Oates finds that these writers have integrated "the warring elements of our culture in themselves, and experience in themselves the evidently 'tragic' personality of the epoch." Writers like Norman Mailer and James Dickey, for example, who she believes "have cheated themselves cruelly of intellectual growth," are dramatizing a "vast, communal tragedy" in their flight from the intellect and attempted return to primitive origins. [19]

Oates feels that Sylvia Plath is the prototypical tragic figure of our age, whose life and death illuminate "the pathological aspects of our era that make a death of the spirit inevitable." She suffered throughout her life from a sense of the isolated ego, the locked-in consciousness which she felt made her an alien in nature. She denigrated her superior intellect, even envied her mute six-month-old infant, and tragically failed to see "that the 'I' of the poet belongs as naturally in the universe as any other aspect of its fluid totality, above all that this 'I' exists in a field of living spirit of which it is one aspect." [20]

Even those writers like Wallace Stevens and Vladimir Nabokov, for whom the "ego emerges as confident and victorious," share in this faulty metaphysics, this fatal dualism, believing that the isolated artist creates art out of his own unique self, cut off from his culture and from nature. [21] Oates discusses the tragedy of the locked-in self, played out in comic extremes, in the works of Samuel Beckett and Eugene Ionesco. In Beckett's work man "the creator of all language . . . is doomed to exist within the confines of his skull, to babble endlessly about the very process of babbling." [22] Ionesco reaches the logical end of existentialism. Not only is Being an "empty fiction," "becoming is a nightmare from which waking is both a salvation and an annihilation." [23]

Joyce Carol Oates does not share this despairing acceptance of nothingness because she does not subscribe to the myth of the isolated artist and the larger myth of the isolated self sustaining it. She writes out of a monistic rather than dualistic philosophical perspective. In her visionary view of the world she sees no necessarily combative relationship between man and nature, the id and the ego, the artist and his culture, good and evil, the instinctive and the intellectual. Rather she sees man and nature, consciousness and unconsciousness, the past and the present, the writer and his culture as all part of a single totality.

Joyce Carol Oates terms her vision "higher humanism, perhaps a kind of intelligent pantheism" which includes within it "all substance in the universe (including the substance fortunate enough to perceive it)." Akin to the American Transcendentalists, her emphasis is less upon man's relationship to nature, more upon the "intelligent pantheism" which binds us into a single family of man. Indeed, in her reading of *Walden* she finds the particulars of nature to be incidental to Thoreau's "real interest," "the attempt of the mind to analyze and control itself," to fuse "the religious impulse and the impulse toward self-analysis" in a quest for the "universality of self."[24] She does not claim to be a mystic. Nor is her vision the singular religious experience accessible only to the saint, but rather it is, she claims, "a logical extension of what we now know," accessible to all people alive to the communal consciousness of our age. Specifically what she sees happening is that scientists and scholars in diverse disciplines are reaching the same monistic truths: "Far from being locked inside our own skins, inside the 'dungeons' of ourselves, we are now able to recognize that our minds belong, quite naturally, to a collective 'mind,' a mind in which we share everything that is mental, most obviously language itself, and that the old boundary of the skin is no boundary at all but a membrane connecting the inner and outer experiences of existence." What was before "mystical vision" is becoming more and more "rational truth." In support of her view she cites the work of cultural anthropologist Claude Lévi-Strauss, to whom anthropology is "part of cosmology"; humanist psychologist Abraham Maslow, who includes mystics as normal or "more-than-normal" human beings rather than dismissing them as irrational; Buckminster Fuller, "who believes that 'human minds and brains may be essential in the total design' of the universe"; R. D. Laing, whom she terms a "Freudian/post-Freudian mystic," who "has set out not only to experience but to articulate a metaphysical 'illumination' whereby self and other become joined"; Sir James Jeans, British physicist/philosopher, who argues that "mind no longer appears as an accidental intruder into the realm of matter; we are beginning to suspect that we ought rather to hail it as the creator and governor of the realm of matter." That all these men are expressing the view "once considered the exclusive property of mystics" proves to Joyce Carol Oates "that the old dichotomy of Reason/Intuition has vanished or is vanishing."[25]

III   A Communal Art

Oates's monistic philosophy shapes her conception of herself as an artist. Since she feels that the intellect is as "natural" to man as the instincts are, she does not scorn civilization, intelligence, "Faustian" control. Indeed, she has said repeatedly that she identifies as an artist with Mann's Adrian Leverkühn. She does not feel that the artist can be "too intellectual":

In our time, in the Seventies, we are chided for being too intellectual, too clinical, if we do not surrender to the tyranny of the Present. Our art, if it is careful, if it makes a rational and even calculated point, is considered a betrayal of the spontaneous joy of life—living—which is always non-rational or anti-rational, as if only the more primitive levels of our brains are truly human. All of this is a mistake. More than that, it is a waste: it is a waste that intelligent people should earnestly deny their intelligence, extolling the impulsive and the sensuous and the "original" . . . and though I believe that the basis of the writing of fiction is the unconscious, the oceanic, ungovernable, unfathomable reservoir of human energy, it is still my deepest certainty that art, if not life, requires intelligence and discretion and transcendence.[26]

But Oates does feel that the myth of the isolated artist has been perpetuated too long, damaging both the creative writers who subscribe to it and the criticism predicated upon it. Oates insists that the artist does not create in isolation, out of his ego, but rather that his art grows out of and is a part of his culture. Like the scientist who acknowledges his debt to others, who knows that his findings are dependent upon the investigations which have come before his, the artist, too, is an individual who attempts "to give voice to many voices," who attempts "to synthesize and explore and analyze." His work should be looked upon as a "communal effort": "If I were to suggest, in utter seriousness, that my fiction is the creation of thousands upon thousands of processes of consciousness, synthesized somehow in me, I would be greeted with astonishment or disbelief, or dismissed as being 'too modest.' In civilization, no one can be 'too modest.' "[27]

What has been thought of by some as feigned modesty or coy disingenuousness is, I think, Oates's genuine respect for both the artist's nurturing by his culture and the inexplicable nature of the creative process. For Oates the artist is both a personal human being and "an impersonal creative process." His talent is a mystery: "why does his era require *him* to give shape to these shapeless dreams?—Why not someone else? A question not to be answered."[28] His inspiration, his consciousness, like that of any man, "is not the private possession of the individual . . . but belongs to his culture."[29] It is not surprising, I think, for a writer of such extraordinary productivity as Oates to be in awe of the creative process. She sees herself, indeed all artists, as a kind of medium who takes in and gives shape to stimuli from her culture. The writer, she feels, is not totally responsible for what he writes about: he must insist upon "the sanctity of the

world. . . . It may be his role, his function, is to articulate the very
worst, to force into consciousness the most perverse and terrifying
possibilities of the epoch, so that they can be dealt with and not
simply feared."[30] But because there "is a pernicious symbiotic
relationship between writers and critics," critics may "condition their
subjects," Oates fears, to write against their own inspiration, to cut
themselves off from the nourishing communal "reservoir of energy"
which infuses their work.[31] Now, although one may sense a defen-
sive plea for immunity from criticism here, nonetheless, this respect
for the sanctity of the artist's world is consistent with Oates's view of
the artist as voice and synthesizer of his culture's consciousness.

Oates argues that just as a writer is part and product of his culture,
he is recipient of its literary and intellectual traditions. Like T. S.
Eliot, she sees the individual talent existing withing a "strong
tradition": "I just see myself as standing in a very strong tradition and
my debt to other writers is very obvious. I couldn't exist without
them."[32] Oates eclectically absorbs images and ideas from other
writers as well as from experiential reality. Profusely interspersed
throughout her books are quotations from and allusions to other
writers' works. Even her titles are often literary allusions. A number
of her stories are rewritings of well-known short-story masterpieces
such as Henry James's "Turn of the Screw," Kafka's "The Metamorphosis," Joyce's "The Dead," and Chekhov's "The Lady with the Pet
Dog." She characterizes these stories as "spiritual marriages" between herself and these literary masters, a tribute to her "kinship"
and her "love and extreme devotion to these other writers."[33] She
even gives credit to an imaginary author, "Ferandes," whose stories
she claims to have "translated" from the Portuguese in *The Poisoned
Kiss*. This alleged "possession" by an alien, imaginary author whose
stories are quite antithetical to her own is Oates's strangest account of
her extraordinary receptivity to stimuli from outside her conscious
self. She is reluctant to isolate influences, claiming, "I've been
influenced in many ways by nearly everyone I've read, and I've read
nearly everyone."[34] Intellectually, she is nurtured by diverse cur-
rents in modern thought.

Oates then is a writer especially sensitive to how much of the
creative process is outside of the conscious control of the artist, how
much is drawn from beyond his own ego. As she would bring the
writer down from his elitist ivory tower, she is impatient with an
art-for-art's sake mentality, an overemphasis on craftsmanship to the

exclusion of "felt life." While Oates admires careful craftsmanship, she also values the writer like D. H. Lawrence whose intense need "to convey the emotions of one man to his fellows" makes his work uneven.[35] In advice to novice writers in an article entitled "Building Tension in a Short Story," Oates argues:

It isn't "words" or "style" that make a scene, but the context behind the words, and the increase of tension as characters come into conflict with one another. "Words" themselves are relatively unimportant, since there are countless ways of saying the same thing.

A final suggestion: be daring, take on anything. Don't labor over little cameo works in which every word is to be perfect. Technique holds a reader from sentence to sentence, but only content will stay in his mind.[36]

Indeed, perhaps the most common charge against her is that she doesn't spend enough time worrying about "words," perfecting her craft. Statements like that above, coupled with her amazing productivity, have created the impression that she does not revise, and although she insists that she does—painstakingly—her style is often not finely honed.

IV *A Participatory Readership*

Oates clearly stresses the rhetorical nature of fiction over its value as crafted art: "all the books published under my name in the past 10 years have been formalized, complex propositions about the nature of personality and its relationship to a specific culture (contemporary America). The propositions are meant to be hypothetical and exploratory, inviting responses that are not simple, thalamic praise/ abuse, but some demonstration that there is an audience that participates in the creation of art."[37] For her, as well as for D. H. Lawrence, the novel is the "one bright book of life," or, as she calls it, "the most human of all art forms,"[38] which expresses truths as no other medium can. Just as writers should not overly invest their egos in their works, their works should not be viewed as "crimes for which they are on perpetual trial."[39] One senses Oates's impatience with the often unsympathetic reception her works have received and her exasperation that they have not elicited the kind of participatory readership that she would like. Her fictional inquiry focuses obsessively upon the nature of the "self" and its relationship to "the other." Although Oates's published canon does not yet span much time, a continuum can be discerned in it, a continual reformulation and reassessment of the problems of selfhood, which shows her characters groping toward the liberating oneness which underlies their creator's vision.

CHAPTER 2

The Apprenticeship: A Lost Eden

J OYCE Carol Oates with her first two published volumes, *By the North Gate* and *Upon the Sweeping Flood,* unequivocally established herself as a masterful storyteller. In these early stories, so often set within the fictional locale Eden County, the back-country world of upper New York State, it seemed as if she were finding her "little postage-stamp world," as William Faulkner found his in Yoknapatawpha County, a fertile milieu that would allow her to dramatize her themes within a recurrent, densely realized setting. The strong sense of people and place gives an authority to these stories that she loses when she abandons this setting in her later fiction. While the themes and motifs dramatized in these stories recur throughout Oates's fiction, they are here skillfully placed in a context which is not just geographical, but ironically symbolical: Eden is lost; the past is irretrievable; moral innocence has been forfeited; the ability to make sense out of experience is elusive.

I By the North Gate: *Confronting Evil and Ennui*

The first and last stories of this volume, "Swamps" and "By the North Gate," are typical presentations of themes repeatedly dramatized in these early collections. Both stories focus on an old man who is confronted with barbarous cruelty and violence. The old man of "Swamps," after caring for a pregnant girl and assisting in the delivery of her child, is assaulted by the young woman and stunned by her murder of her own baby. The old man of "By the North Gate" is taunted by malicious boys who set his field on fire and murder his dog. But the two old men have had very different lives and respond in very different ways to the upsetting confrontations with mindless evil. "Swamps," while told in third person, is filtered through the perspective of a young boy who admires his independent, skillful, respected grandfather, whose joyful optimism contrasts with his father's cynicism. Old man Revere of "By the North Gate," in contrast, is much less sure of the goodness of life, much less in control of himself and experience. Just as he is discouraged by the ramshackle state of his farm, by the weeds which he has spent sixty-eight years fighting and never managing to subdue, he is similarly dispirited by his failure to affix a lasting meaning to life: "All my life I done battle against it: that life don't mean nothin'! That it don't make sense! Sixty-eight years of a battle" (p. 206).[1]

But Revere finds in himself the strength to endure the trauma created by the vicious boys while the grandfather is broken by the girl's ingratitude and inhumanity. Perhaps Oates is suggesting that Revere has been tempered by his sixty-eight-year struggle against chaos and nothingness, whereas the grandfather has never directly encountered evil in his successful ventures in the "goddam, good world." Old man Revere refuses to generalize from his experience with the senseless cruelty of the boys: "They don't stand for anything s'post to change my mind about life" (p. 207). He envisions the boys "caught within the accidental patterns of a fate in which he himself would be caught" (p. 207). Although the old man is exhausted by his futile struggle for intellectual comprehension of life, yet the story ends on a note of affirmation as he remembers the one period in his life—when he had had long talks with the schoolteacher—which "seemed good to remember just the same, good to remember" (p. 208). While their discussions were inconclusive and only partially recalled by the old man, this fledgling attempt at some understanding of life's complexities sustains him against total despair.

The grandfather of "Swamps," in contrast, a broken man after his shattering experience, whines, "They robbed me. . . . They robbed me" (p. 20). Since the woman took only a knife and some pennies, the boy and his father cannot understand the old man's statement, but clearly he has been robbed of his vision of the world and of people as basically good. His belated initiation into evil, into the depths of life-denying contemptuous hate, dispels his joy and optimism. When he recognizes man's capacity for inhuman depravity, he loses his Eden and his ability to recollect with pleasure the "good old days." This story, along with "By the North Gate" and many others, suggests that a better past is irretrievably lost. Mindless evil is embodied in the form of young people: the pregnant girl, the vicious boys. Vitality has gone out of life for the grandfather's son just as it has gone out of the farm for old man Revere. Oates is compassionate and insightful in her poignant portrayal of the anxieties of these inarticulate country people, fixed within a familiar but increasingly disquieting environment, and incapable of understanding the emotional complexity of themselves and others.

The same themes are dramatized in stories about younger people in "In the Old World" and "Sweet Love Remembered." In the first Swan Walpole is disturbed by the evil he finds not in others but in himself, and he vainly seeks to purge it through Old Testament punishment—literally seeks to have another exact from him an eye for an eye. The specific incident is left vague: Swan has apparently cut the eye of a Negro youth at a church picnic, and he comes to town seeking the sheriff, hoping in his inarticulate and confused way to be relieved of his burden of guilt by offering the boy his knife to maim his own eye in retaliation. The deputy sheriff tries to assure Swan that "it doesn't matter," implying that the same standards of justice do not apply to blacks and whites. The boy himself, Chaparall, who is in the deputy's custody, is seemingly more amused by the light color of Swan's hair than interested in retaliation or in the moral complexities with which he is struggling. But Swan, like the grandfather of "Swamps," has lost his Eden. In his confusion he conjectures about the first settlers who came to America hoping to start anew, but the problem was that they could not purge themselves clean: "This was no new world to them; this was the old world still. When they came they made it old. . . . Even with all time ahead, it won't get any different, will it?" (p. 158). Similarly, Swan cannot restore his own innocence and make his world pure and explicable. He remains a lonely and confused young man, enveloped by disquieting feelings and depressed by his inability to pull together his fragmentary insights.

Another lonely young person who longs for a sweeter past and laments a lost purity and innocence is the girl in "Sweet Love Remembered," who works as a waitress in a summer resort. She has not, like Swan, committed any particular sin or wrongdoing, yet she recognizes at a very early age that she is corrupted by "the vulgarity and the cheapness of what she saw about her, and her own surrender to it, a sadness of a sweet and alluring force, a tragic, inevitable surrender to the prodding of the loud world" (p. 57). She lives on two levels, conforming on one to the present with a mechanical waitress-smile, the "brittle splendor of an artifice contrived with care before mirrors, postured and grimacing before mirrors, endless mirrors" (p. 57)—but on the other nostalgically contemplating the past and its difference from her present degradation. Recalling her early adoles-

cence, she realizes now that "she loved her brother and that she had
never told him so, that she would never tell him so; she would not be
able to" (p. 59). Her relationship with a morose middle-aged man who
is obsessed with life's transcience and meaninglessness moves her
even farther along the road of disillusionment, "as though some part
of her life was over" (p. 63).

In another story, "The Census Taker," a man is overcome by the
absurdity and inconsequentiality of his occupation. Here, as so often
in Oates's stories, a person's conception of the world is shaken by his
encounter with people totally different from himself. At the end of his
round one day, he is unnerved by two children—a boy who asks blunt
questions and a deeply cynical girl. To the boy's "What you goin' to
ask Pa?," the census taker politely responds: "A number of questions. . . . Nothing important" (p. 25). The boy smartly retorts: "How
come you do it, then?" Such questions, reinforced by the sister's
impassioned, contemptuous ravings, profoundly disturb this quiet
and contained man. The girl has apparently been crazed by the
traumatizing, meaningless events which have shaped their lives.
Their grandmother died of painful cancer; twin brothers also died,
one killed when a tractor accidentally ran over him; their father, hit
on the head by a log, wandered away years ago, never to return to the
family. She is understandably spiteful of a census which attempts to
codify life into simple statistics. To her, nothing is beyond the cruel
and inexplicable "washing away" to which they have been subjected
and to which the census taker himself is not immune: "All washed
away! An' one day a man comin' here spost to be on a census. An' he
don't know how there ain't no census, there ain't nothin', as soon as he
left that-there town called Oriskany it all up an' left, all washed away!
An' them people in the book, all washed away that he thought he
caught an' could keep still, by writin' down. You got your own life in
there mister? What are you? What are you?" (pp. 29–30). It is all that
the census taker can do to leave the house. When the mother asks him
why he did not complete his questioning, he blurts out all the disgust
with himself and his occupation that this encounter has provoked:
"Do you expect me to give you answers? Who am I to give you
answers, to give you anything? Am I a man? Do I look like a man?" (p.
30).

Some stories take place outside of the Eden County setting, but
they are thematically related to the others. One, depicting a campus
party at the University of Wisconsin, "The Expense of Spirit," focuses
on a young English instructor, anxious over his wife's recent deser-

tion. Dissatisfied and ill at ease with the other partygoers, he becomes fascinated with a young, naive, impressionable girl, a student in his class, who is escorted to the party by an attractive black man. At first overawed with what she takes to be the sophisticated world of academia, she is later appalled by the cynicism and nastiness of the group. The story ends with her being drunkenly and desperately pursued by both her young instructor and her black escort, who are apparently taken with the attractiveness of the girl's innocence and naiveté and its contrast with their blighted world of experience and disillusionment.

The same theme is used in a much better story—in fact, one of Oates's finest—"Pastoral Blood," which portrays a girl from a well-to-do family who, shortly before she is to be married, decides that she no longer has a desire to live. She withdraws all of her money from her bank account, buys and puts on cheap clothes, and goes on a careless spree, picking up a companion and stopping at cheap restaurants and bars in little country towns. Although she has seemingly all the advantages, she has no ability to feel or care; she shares the ennui of the other characters in this volume. The detached, slightly mocking narrative voice contributes to the vivid rendering of this girl as the very embodiment of the American ideal:

For twenty years the sun had slanted through the window, illuminating her mirror. Altar of her triumphs, it could do no more than give back to her the certainty of her beauty, her good fortune—child of happiness! Not for her the pillow-choked anguish of thin-legged, hairy-legged girls with acne-ravaged faces, eyes intense and desperate behind glasses. Not for her the dawdling in girlish groups, drifting back from the library alone: a professor's kind of praise to keep them going. Yet professors had noticed Grace too—did they recognize something in her, something beautifully American? (p. 85)

In fact, in this passage and elsewhere in the story, Oates effectively uses the mirror, television, or commercial image as a metaphor for the glossy surface and the hollow essence of Grace, who can even joke about her predictable, clichéd character and appearance. She tells a stranger: "I know you've seen me before. . . . A comic book or movie or television show." She's the cheerleader dancing with her boyfriend, sponsored by shampoo or cereal, who dies but "there is a miracle or something" and when the coffin is reopened, all there is is "a tag with string on it, the kind to loop over buttons. It says 'Size 9–10, Guaranteed Wash and Wear' " (p. 83).

At the end of the story, because of a car accident and her

convalescence in a hospital, she is restored to her family, her fiancé, and her old image, but she is merely coyly waiting for a chance to escape again as the chillingly cynical final paragraph reveals:

Out of the mirror Grace watches the family scene, sees smiles, teeth, blinkings, exchange of glances, uncrossing and crossing of legs. Optimism as healthy and American as the pimples on Brother's forehead and chin. Most of all Grace sees the girl's clever eyes that mirror the germ of enthusiasm, shy feigned germ of love. Now the scene moves away. Slowly back, slowly into the distance. Movie screen, television screen, the dial about to be flicked off. At the last instant the girl glances to the mirror again, seeks reassurance from Grace, gets reassurance. All the time in the world, and the next time there will be no failure. In another year, perhaps. Experience is the best teacher. (pp. 91–92)

Grace has temporarily capitulated to the seemingly Edenic world she had abandoned. There she again projects an image of a privileged, wholesome, innocent American girl, but the narrator reveals with bitter irony the brittle fragility of that world and that image. Oates has written here, early in her career, the kind of story at which she will repeatedly excel, a story which with scalpellike precision exposes the intolerable vacuousness in which so many women find themselves suspended.

II   Upon the Sweeping Flood: *Search for Order through Violence,*
"Blood Bondage," or Love

Less often set in Eden County than the stories in *By the North Gate,* those in *Upon the Sweeping Flood* embody some of the same themes: the gropings of inarticulate people for order and meaning and the discovery of hidden, unlovely depths of passion or of emptiness within one's self. The emphasis here, however, is more focused on the interrelationships among people, be they familial, emotional, or social. Oates exhibits here the beginning of her intense preoccupation with both the tenacious bonds of the family and the mysterious emotions of love.

"Norman and the Killer," like several other stories in this volume, depicts a character who tries to order and fix experience through violence. Until he is thirty, Norman lives a quiet, conventional, but unfulfilled life. The conflict of the story is precipitated by his chance encounter with a gasoline attendant who Norman is sure was his brother's murderer many years ago. He becomes obsessed with this man, unable to act normally with his girl friend Ellen, indeed, in effect, destroying their relationship even though he desperately would like to cling to her as protection "against the violence of the past" (p. 117).[2] He feels that his fate is locked inevitably to this man, that he must be the avenger of his brother's death, and that this burden makes it impossible for him ever to be normal and live in the ordinary world.

This forsaking of any attempt to live a conventional life frees Norman and gives license to violence: "He had never before felt quite so free: the immensity of freedom to act and to act entirely without consequence" (p. 119). He goes back to the gasoline station, forces the man at gunpoint to get into the car, takes him to an abandoned shanty, and attempts to get him to confess his guilt. This extended grilling of the man casts doubts on Norman's unshaking conviction that he is the killer. The man appears genuinely ignorant of the crime; he is willing finally to confess merely to escape the clutches of this seeming madman. Norman sees the ploy and will not accept it, but he apparently does not see his own distortions of the truth. In his falsifying memories he idealizes his brother in a way which conflicts sharply with the truth, making him into the older brother he wished he had had—big, protective, intelligent, close to him. In truth, he was small, insecure, desirous of quitting school, and as bored with his brother's companionship as Norman was with his: "The two of them . . . were doomed to be brothers forever and could do nothing about it" (pp. 114–15). Norman needs to believe in this lost, ideal brother; it simplifies the complexities of life, takes the burden of guilt for his own shortcomings off of himself, and places them on his brother's killer. Like Swan of "In the Old World," he believes or hopes that "justice" will restore the lost order of the world: "Nothing can be right and balanced again until justice is won—the injured party has to have justice" (p. 127).

All of his dissatisfactions build up and pour out; the unfortunate gasoline attendant becomes the scapegoat for all Norman's invective against a world of unpunished, ubiquitous killers: "Dirty bastards, killers, a whole world of killers" (p. 131). He lets his prisoner go and shoots after him as he attempts his escape; it is unclear whether he kills him or not. Norman feels "the numbed, beatific emptiness of one who no longer doubts that he possesses the truth, and for whom life will have forever lost its joy" (p. 132). But the "truth" he really possesses is a recognition of his isolation and alienation. He is the "killer" in his world; his own failure to secure his identity will inevitably kill off any potential communion with others.

Dr. Carl Reeves of "The Survival of Childhood" shares Norman's insecurity and vague sense of failure while living a seemingly normal, successful life as a married college instructor in an industrial city. Like Norman, his latent insecurity is tied up with his relationship with a brother, Gene, who at age twenty-nine still lives at home in the poverty-stricken country of their youth. Although Carl appears to be the successful one, who had "escaped the curse of his family, bad luck inherited with stubbornness, opaqueness, an inability or refusal to understand the world" (p. 31), he is still jealous and intimidated, as he was as a child, by his more vital, self-assured brother. Carl had thought that he had succeeded in severing all bonds with his past and his family, but he is not free from the "terrific force" of "blood bondage" (p. 38). Through his brother's turmoil and ultimate suicide, he learns that he is profoundly shaped—both sustained and limited—by his complex relationship with him.

Gene writes to Carl and, when he receives no answer, comes to his office in a brusque and awkward attempt to institute the brotherly communication that has been lacking. Gene is disquieted by a recurring dream in which he envisions an unknown woman. He suspects that he is going crazy and seeks reassurance from his brother. Carl, "with his early, neurotic sensitivity, his awe and fear of the world" (p. 35), cannot imagine that his simple, fearless brother has the capacity for insanity ("You don't have the right kind of mind for it" [p. 36]), but he learns later how completely he has misunderstood and underestimated his brother's sensitivity and behavior.

Reluctantly responding to "blood bondage" Carl visits his family shortly after Gene's visit: "he must return to them, endure them, so that he might finally be free" (p. 39). But unknown to Carl, Gene has already made the decision to commit suicide. All he tells Carl is that he has discovered who the woman in the photograph is, a cousin of their grandmother, now dead and buried along with her four children. The next morning he joins his distant cousin by putting a bullet through his head. Upon opening his brother's locked bedroom, Carl is shocked to discover the degree of disturbance and tortuous compassion revealed in the "galaxy of faces" which Gene had drawn on his bedroom walls. Carl discovers that Gene was not the failure as a man that he and everyone took him to be; he was, in fact, admirable, a person who returned home not because his "savage energy had burned itself out" (p. 47), but because with his "fatal sensitivity" he felt a compassion and responsibility for the people there. He was consumed by "angry sympathy . . . forlorn, raging despair for the horror of life at this edge of the world" (p. 48). Carl realizes the extent of his own guilt, his failure to love and to understand his brother. He has had, in truth, the ideal brother whom Norman erroneously imagines he has lost. For his brother had possessed a generosity of spirit which Carl both misunderstood and could not duplicate.

Indeed, neither brother escapes the deterministic influences of place and family. Carl's dedication to getting away from "the horror of life at this edge of the world" and from the "terrific force" of "blood bondage" has maimed him, has made him incapable of the depth of love and feeling which Gene could stifle only through an act of self-destructive violence. Carl's wife is bitterly disappointed in their noncommunicative marriage and their failure to produce a child, a barrenness which has psychological implications in this potent story. Gene has been the sacrificial victim of his brother's success, but Carl has not "survived" childhood with his selfhood intact. Oates has written a number of subsequent stories which similarly expose the emotional inadequacies of the intellectually adept "survivor."

Another story with this theme, "Archways," centers on Klein, a "nervous young man" whose most characteristic emotion is shame. He is ashamed of his poverty, his poor clothes, his age (at twenty-nine he is several years older than his fellow graduate students), his parents, his background, even "his shame itself" (p. 148). He "imitated others," reading books, writing papers, studying, and teaching the hopeless students in his remedial English classes who had been "educated now into knowing their unworth" (p. 150), but, unable to generate any enthusiasm for living, he gets satisfaction only out of the contemplation of his own suicide.

But his life is changed by the chance encounter and subsequent relationship with one of his students, a girl as miserably lonely, anonymous, disappointed, and cut off from "the enemy, that great impersonal block of humanity whose surfaces were slick and impenetrable" (p. 158), as he is himself. Through her love he becomes infused with a new enthusiasm; he enjoys "the power of his new freedom. He had been loved. He had been worthy of love" (p. 163), but his interest in her as a person wanes. Obsessed with his new interest in his scholarship, his appearance, and his future, and brimming with a new-found vitality, he dashes off a note to her which, although kindly intended, is a cruel dismissal. She drops out of his class and he gives little thought to her again except when he troubles over and finally records an "F" as her final grade.

In an extremely caustic final paragraph, the omniscient narrator sums up his undistinguished, predictable future. Klein achieves "as well as any of the second-best students" (p. 164). By committing much to memory and by being "grateful for and humble to the great academic tradition in which he would live out his life," he becomes a married, anonymous, comfortable teacher at a "not well-known little college," who is indifferent about and ungrateful to the pathetic girl who changed his life through her love: "What possibility of happiness without some random, incidental death?"

The failure of love and compassion is also the theme of an excellent story, "Stigmata," with a unique subject—alleged sainthood. Mr. Turner, a patient at St. Jerome's Home for the Aged, has the year before experienced wounds which bled on Good Friday. Now as Good Friday approaches again, five of his six children, the press, the hospital and clerical staff, and the public anxiously await the recurrence of this "miracle." The third-person point of view of the story is filtered through the perspective of Walt, a less successful, skeptical, and sometimes openly cynical son, who wishes that he could communicate with his brothers and sisters, but who feels that they share their father's self-deception and emotional dishonesty. The other children, unlike Walt, having idealized their memories of their father, are ready to believe in his sainthood. Clara, in particular, is desperate not only for the miracle but for some special confirmation of their relationship as father and daughter, some interest in her as a person.

The miracle does not go exactly according to expectations. The bleeding starts on Thursday rather than Friday, but as one priest explains, "God's time is not necessarily our time" (p. 17). But neither does the bleeding stop on schedule; it continues on Easter Sunday, upsetting everyone. When the father murmurs to Walt, "I hurt," the son understands, as no one else does, that his father is being designated a sinner, not a saint, being punished for his lifelong detachment from the world. The "august generous indifference, that godly calm that stifles all anger, all love" (p. 12), has been a mask that has cut him off from human involvement. He has lived in a false Eden, an unholy void: "Safe in his old age, before that safe in his tranquility, he had refined himself out of life—he had had, so easily, six children; he had given them nothing, not his own identity, not identities of their own, he had not distinguished one from the other;

he had moved as a ghost among the mild, ghostly illusions of this world as a young man, and, now, as an old man; he had never been a man; and he was being educated now in the pain of being human" (pp. 24–25).

Oates, like D. H. Lawrence, uses blood to depict the life of the emotions. Mr. Turner must bleed now since physicality impinges irrevocably upon all, including those who cerebrally would refine themselves out of existence. Through his benign indifference, Mr. Turner has failed truly to duplicate Christ's love and compassion and now he must suffer his torment.

At his recognition of his father's situation, Walt goes into a fit of anger, pouring out his resentment against this father who failed to reciprocate love. Eventually quieted with an injection, he is not allowed to visit his father again, and he hears from a stranger a few days later of the father's suicide. Although this man tries to explain the act as a consequence of intolerable pain, Walt insists, "My father was responsible for what he did" (p. 26). But Walt has difficulty assessing his father's "legacy of death, spiteful death, but a work of art!" (pp. 26-27). Indeed, he shares in his father's final bitter skepticism. As he examines his hands, he finds no wounds, no scars, no blisters; "clean as a life never quite lived," no different from the innocent hands he had looked on idly as a child. Like his father, like Grace of "Pastoral Blood" and several other characters, he is locked in a false, vacuous Eden. His tragedy is that his intellectual understanding of his situation does not carry with it the ability to effect any change. Like Carl, who "survived" childhood, he is destined to be an incomplete person, one whose emotional isolation will always undermine his intellectual competence.

Another character who shares Mr. Turner's self-deceptive mask of benevolence and calm and who experiences an epiphanic self-revelation of his unlovely inner self is Walter Stuart, the successful businessman who attempts in "Upon the Sweeping Flood" to be a good samaritan by returning to a flooded area to rescue the stranded. But where Mr. Turner discovers his own emptiness, Walter Stuart learns of his uncivilized depths, his capacity for brutal violence. He attempts to rescue two stranded back-country adolescents, a coarse, foul-mouthed eighteen-year-old girl and her thirteen-year-old brother, who mumbles hysterically about his lost horse and a benevolent God and who is subject to periodic seizures of insanity. Since the flood waters are too high for his car, Stuart must struggle with the teenagers in their house, and he curses the foolhardy impulse that got him into this fix. His wife, children, and orderly, refined life seem increasingly remote and intangible. He would like to think of himself as in control: the intelligent, rational mind, the "sane circle of quiet carefully preserved inside the chaos of the storm—that the three were safe within the sanctity of this circle; this was how man always conquered nature, how he subdued things greater than himself" (p. 217), but he has less influence on the chaos than the chaos does on him. He begins to question the life he has led until now: "Perhaps he had blundered out of his way, drawn into the wrong life, surrendered to the wrong role. . . . He only now sensed the incompleteness of his former life" (pp. 217–18). Again, the Eden County setting functions as an integral part of the story, thematically and symbolically. Stuart's return to the country of his youth, like Carl's in "The Survival of Childhood," reveals to him the incompleteness of his "escape" and the hollowness of his carefully groomed respectability.

When the house is washed away, they float along on the roof until the waters begin to subside and they can land on a hill. Stuart is overwhelmed by this experience and his inevitable inability to communicate its vividness and significance to his family and friends. It has turned him "into a different person, a stranger even to himself" (p. 221). When the boy recovers from one of his seizures and the day returns, Stuart is troubled by the sameness of things; only he has changed. He sees this return to conventional order as a mockery. What he has learned is "that the God of these people had indeed arranged things, had breathed the order of chaos into forms, had animated even Stuart himself forty years ago" (p. 223). He wants to perpetuate the chaos, embrace it, rather than return to normal. Impulsively he lashes out at the boy, striking him on the head with a rotted limb and attempting to drown him in the flood waters. He is about to attack the girl as well when she shrewdly points out to him the approach of the rescuers. Wading out into the shallow waters, Stuart cries out, "Save me! Save me!" when they arrive. They will apparently save him from the brutal savagery unleashed in himself, but he is unlikely to be the same disciplined, orderly person he was before. Oates shows that a seething emotional core lies dormant in even the most quiescent people. All of her writing is indeed about the "mystery of human emotions," as she observes in a comment that prefaces paperback editions of several of her works.

Where Stuart's self-revelation is precipitated by his encounter with the coarse humanity of lower-class people and by the chaos of the flood, the woman of "First Views of the Enemy" tries to protect her son and herself from such people and their latent threat to her well-being and material security. This vividly realized, caustic story opens with her nearly hitting a small boy with her car as he darts from the swarming multitude of disorderly, boisterous Mexican children who play around their disabled bus. She is shaken both by the near-accident and by the attitude of the mocking, envious children and adults who temporarily block the exit of her car from the scene.

She speeds home, disquieted by her son's reserve, by the awakening of unpleasant memories about her reluctant motherhood and emotionally unserene life, and by the seeming threat of the migrant workers. As they turn up their drive, she thinks how foolish they have been to live so far out of town, how vulnerable they are to attack. Attempting to remain calm, she yet becomes increasingly apprehensive as she lovingly surveys her possessions: "In all directions her possessions stretched out about her, defining her, identifying her, and they were vulnerable and waiting, the dirt road led right to them" (p. 84). She begins securing her middle-class fortress, pulling the draperies, locking the windows and doors, even clipping her beautiful roses in such a distracted hurry that "dozens of bleeding scratches" appear on her hands. Quickly arranging them in a vase, she thinks: "Beauty, beauty—it was necessary to have beauty, to possess it, to keep it around oneself!—how well she understood that now" (p. 86). Then, in an attempt to draw her son to herself, she hastily scavenges the refrigerator and pulls out food to eat, including strawberry tarts. Ravenously hungry, she herself begins devouring the tarts. Finally breaking his reserve and sharing her mood, Timmy smiles before biting the tart and says, "*He* can't hit the car again, it's all locked up" (p. 88). "Eat, *Eat,*" his loving mother urges as they gorge themselves on their gastronomic opulence, selfishly secured from the grubby hands of the poor. Here again is the fragile, materialistic paradise which substitutes for a lost Eden for so many Oatesian characters.

The effective irony of the story is complemented by the skillful use of the motif of red. The blood of the child which *almost* spilled on the road—the bloody connection to "real" life from which they retreat into their sanctuary—is recalled by the blood-red dirt of the road which leads to their door, by the red car which remains unsullied by humanity, by the beautiful red roses which Annette tries to secure from the gaze of migrant workers, by the blood which appears on her hands while desperately gathering them, by the red lawn furniture and red swivel chair which accent their elegant exterior and interior decoration, and by the red tarts which they gluttonously expropriate to themselves. Annette and Timmy have been spared the bloody initiation or the violent assault which so often alters the lives of other Oatesian characters, but revealed is the terrible sacrifice they pay—the emotional constraint, the suppressed hysteria and terror, which are concomitant with their sterile, affluent, selfish lives. The achievement of Joyce Carol Oates in these first two volumes is considerable. In fact, in my opinion, she has not in later volumes brought together so many fine stories as she does here. She demonstrates a grasp of her subjects and her craft in a way she does not always exhibit when she leaves behind Eden County and its backcountry people and experiments with more innovative short-story forms. These stories are, moreover, imbued with compassion as well as insight, often evoking a resonance and depth of feeling which many of the later flat and clinical stories lamentably lack. Nonetheless, that Oates refuses merely to duplicate what she has already achieved is a credit to her ambition and talent.

In some ways, however, Oates's work is duplicative, in that she obsessively focuses on the same aspects of human experience, dramatizing again and again the deterministic influence of environment and family. "The mystery of human emotions" is intimately bonded with complex geographical, sociological, economic, and especially familial ties. The "terrific force" of "blood bondage"—the parent-child and sibling relationships that indeliably shape one's selfhood—is something that Oates respects and repeatedly explores. The disorienting, frightening, sometimes ennobling, sometimes debasing power of love and sex and the entangling relationships produced by these explosive forces are at the center of most of Oates's subsequent fiction. Violence—whether as a release from intolerable emotional pressure or as an attempt to simplify or to rebel against the incomprehensible and meaningless or as an attempt to create a bond to another person or as a gratuitous and sadistic act—is a subject that continues to fascinate Joyce Carol Oates. She explores both cognitive and actual violence, both contained and uncontrolled emotional duress, with an intensity unusual in any writer. Her later work becomes almost uncomfortably a study in disturbed behavior, but in these volumes she reveals how close the seemingly normal person is to being a victim or a perpetrator of violence, how thin is the veneer of civilized behavior. And in presenting those characters who manage to keep the veneer intact and the emotions in control, she is devastating in her revelation of the toll that this emotional suppression extracts—emptiness, inhibition, frigidity, or insecurity. Indeed, perhaps the most common Oatesian theme is the loneliness and isolation of the individual barred from emotional communion with others, a condition which is especially painful when it is coupled, as it so often is, with an inability to make any sense out of experience, to gain any intellectual ascendancy over life's seeming meaninglessness. Whether her canvas is the novel or the short story, Oates's fiction never strays very far from these same thematic concerns. Similarily, many motifs which run through these stories—such as blood and disease, media and mirror images, food and opulent furnishings—become familiar trappings of Oates's work, enhancing the importance of these masterful apprenticeship stories.

III   With Shuddering Fall: *Study of Innocence*

Joyce Carol Oates's first novel, *With Shuddering Fall,* is more ambitious and ultimately less satisfactory as a work than the early collections of stories even though it examines many of the same themes much more intensively. It, too, is set within Eden County, although the central characters, Shar and Karen, leave this world of their childhood for the transient life of the racetrack circuit. "Eden" continues to function symbolically as well as literally; the novel is most centrally a study in the nature of innocence.

Destined to be lovers, Shar and Karen are diametrically opposed personalities whose attachment and antagonism generate the conflicts of the novel. Seventeen-year-old Karen Herz, the younger daughter of a dominant, dictatorial father, is dependently attached to her father, her religion, and her home. A high-school dropout, she has no interest in men, no desire to get married and to leave her family. She listens with fascination to her father's Bible readings, captivated by the story of Abraham and Isaac, envious of the prescribed plotting of one's life "manipulated by God Himself! It was a queer thought and Karen did not really understand it, though she felt very clearly the power of its attraction" (p. 34).[3] She longs for a similar "absolution of this life." She gets her wish, but it is concomitant with traumatizing experiences. The son of a neighbor, Shar, tricks her into accompanying him to town. He makes sexual advances; she retaliates by involving them in an accident. He in turn lies to her father about her motives, precipitating a brutal fight between the two men. As he lies bleeding on the ground, her father demands: "Don't come to me until you get him. Kill him. Kill him" (p. 50). Like Isaac,

Karen acquiesces to self-sacrifice in obedient fulfillment of her
father's command. But rather than simply mounting the sacrificial
pyre, she takes the circuitous route of offering herself sexually to
Shar, traveling with him on the racetrack circuit, and awaiting her
opportunity to effect the retributive death.

While Karen longs to cement the bond to her father and home,
Shar desperately tries to sever it. At the beginning of the novel he
reluctantly returns home to minister to his dying father, but, unable
to curb the rebellious instincts which this return engenders, he
angrily sets his father's shack on fire, seeking to free himself through
destruction from "a life of order, of meticulous, heart-straining
order!" (p. 173).

Both central characters have a yearning for self-control and unity,
but they construe them differently, postulating a Christian versus
pagan world-view. Karen seeks essentially to nullify her existence by
her identification within a hierarchical order: "Karen realized she had
no existence without the greater presence of someone to acknowledge her (her father, God)" (p. 111). Shar seeks to achieve his
selfhood through closer identification with the sensuous world:
" 'God, how I love this world!' Shar muttered fiercely. 'A damn good
world! I can't get close enough to it—' " (p. 138). Only in the "world
apart," the intense and simplified world of the racetrack, is he "safe
from entanglements with anyone—with himself, even, his usual self,
the mortality in him that linked him to other men. He would be safe
from time, lifted above time, he would be free of human bondage" (p.
84). But, just as he broke up Karen's idyllic world, this bondage to her
upsets his "simplicity of vision, and simplicity of emotion." The two
become involved in a life-and-death struggle for mastery and control,
a battle that Karen wins because her nullity gives her greater strength
than Shar's passion.

In passages much reminiscent of D. H. Lawrence, Oates describes
the infatuation and repulsion, the struggle for power and control
underlying their sexual relationship. Until meeting Karen, Shar had
prided himself for his machinelike precision of control, the "oiled and
clicking parts of his being. . . had run him for years, had initiated him
to a pattern of reacting and understanding that was now being
violated" (p. 115), but Karen is much more controlled and much less
moved by their relationship. She "had not abandoned anything of
herself and so was in a way protected" (p. 116). Their relationship is
merely a "game of some sort" and Shar does not know the rules: "It
was Karen's icy reserve that controlled the game, precisely the secret

in her that commanded her degradation" (p. 117). "One day Shar abandoned the game" (p. 117), but Karen does not and cannot. Shar is frightened and confused by the lack of self-control his surrender entails. In Lawrentian terms, he is opening himself up to the loss of self that must precede birth to a new self in the "baptism of fire in passion." But like so many of Lawrence's women, Karen's soul contracts, refuses to participate in this potential communion: "Karen closed her eyes and felt her soul contract itself into a tiny pebble-like thing safe in her brain" (p. 121). Although she can acknowledge the reality of Shar's passion, it only makes her hate him more completely. Frustrated by her holding back, Shar would like to destroy her in murderous spite.

But although death seems to be the only way out of his intolerable infatuation and his inability to break through to a liberating communion, Shar cannot vent his rage on Karen; he must destroy himself instead. As if to seal the inevitable choice of death, Karen in their last act of lovemaking has a miscarriage, having failed to warn Shar that she is pregnant. Repelling Shar's solicitations, she quells the self that would respond to him and pronounces, in effect, his death sentence, "You make me sick" (p. 181). The final race is the climax of the struggle between the lovers, and for both, Shar's death is a victory and a release; Shar goes to his death fulfilled, having achieved finally his pagan selfhood, whereas Karen's Christian victory is empty and it precipitates a mental breakdown.

Max, Shar's racetrack promoter, "a bloated, insatiable spectator, a product of a refined civilization" (p. 143), gets vicarious pleasure out of Shar's dangerous courting of death on the racetrack, his "inhuman control of himself," and his "childlike innocence." Max is convinced that Shar is a passive recipient of life's fortunes: "He is the child who does nothing, to whom all things are done. Whatever happens to him he hasn't deserved or earned—good or bad—whatever—these things simply happen, accidents" (p. 125). He envies this state of innocence "beyond good and evil" which is inaccessible to all but the childlike: "What brilliance there is in a child, who takes the world as chaos and never thinks about it. *There* is innocence—it is impossible in anyone else, in anyone who believes" (p. 126). Alluding to Milton's *Paradise Lost,* he claims that the problem with people who have lost their innocence is that they expect things to get better as they do in literature, but in reality, there is no paradise; it is better to be childlike, to have no expectations, to assume no responsibility. Shar has indeed been "innocent" throughout his life, incapable of pulling together the fragments of his being, incapable of assuming responsibility for himself and his actions, incapable of penetrating through "the fine invisible barrier that separated him from other people, from the world, from reality" (p. 184). But in spite of Max's envious adulation of such a state, nothing is blissful about it. In the terms of Kierkegaard's *Sickness unto Death,* Shar's ignorance of good and evil carries with it "the despairing unconsciousness of having a self." He is a finite man reaching for the infinite; he seeks with Karen communion with a world beyond his anonymous self, beyond the "fine invisible barrier." But denied liberation through love, he achieves it through death. Moments before his death he "falls" from innocence to experience. For the first time in his life he experiences guilt, and it gives him a sense of control over his fate unexperienced before: "Shar's heart pounded with the excitement that he had finally transcended the fragments of his anonymity. . . . He knew who he was, he knew exactly what he was doing, and why; he was guilty—completely guilty—and his guilt, like his love, had pulled him together" (p. 185). He experiences an exhilarating sense of freedom, the freedom that Kierkegaard (admittedly within a Christian context which is absent here) holds to be concomitant with a fall to experience: "to be guilty means precisely to be individually responsible. This implies freedom, and freedom annuls the concept of fate."[4]

Although Karen had her own purposes in sending Shar to his death, she also understands that his death was an affirming act, a way to triumph over accident: "his life was an accident but his death wasn't—he made his death for himself! He was a man!" (p. 191). Recognizing the inevitability of death and joyfully embracing it, Shar attempts to remove all impediments such as gloves, helmet, and goggles "that disguised him, denied him humanity; he hated the shock absorbers, the fireproof clothing, the devices invented for safety's sake—as if there were any protection possible against mortality" (p. 185–86). His "shuddering fall" also echoes the end of the George Meredith poem "Ode to the Spirit of Earth in Autumn," from which the title of the novel is taken:

> Bacchante Mother! stern to those
> Who live not in thy heart of mirth;
> Death shall I shrink from, loving thee?
> Into the breast that gives the rose,
>   Shall I with shuddering fall?[5]

As the poet awaits the "dark to-be," and longs to embrace joyfully his "Bacchante Mother!" "Great Mother Nature!" so too Shar anticipates his violent communion with the natural world that he has always loved.

Max is correct in his assessment of Shar's innocence, but he erroneously thinks that Karen shares in it. He is more correct when he intuitively suspects a correspondence between himself and Karen. Both vicariously draw their lives from others. Both use Shar for their own purposes. Max is the epicure who feasts intellectually on the vital life experienced by Shar; Karen is the dutiful daughter who plots her victory over her lover to secure her father's favor. Obviously she is not innocent in the sense that Max uses the term; she does not view events as accidental, life as chaotic; she is not without either expectations or responsibility. She is only innocent in the sense that she never *personalizes* that responsibility. She willingly surrenders herself "to claims of blood and duty," but her "soul" in itself "had no existence" (p. 111). She is incapable of a self-directed act, an act without the sanction of a father or a God.

For Karen too Shar's death brings communion, but it is a hollow one. After her sojourn and recovery in a mental hospital, she is returned to her father and her religion. She is returned, in effect, to the Eden she has lost, but she now sees, as she did not before, its lack of innocence. The final scene of the novel takes place fittingly in a church where Christ's sacrifice re-created in the celebration of the Mass seemingly dwarfs what Karen has given up for her father: "Here is a real sacrifice, her father might say, pointing up to the altar. You think you have given yourself, you think you have been fed upon— and so in a way you have—but still you are alive, you have health and youth and beauty" (p. 222). But as Friedrich Nietzsche in "Beyond Good and Evil" lambasts the "anti-natural" cruelty of the practice of Christian and prehistoric religions to sacrifice the first-born to the gods, so too Oates's emphasis is on the emptiness of Karen's Isaaclike sacrifice to preserve the authoritarian structures of family and religion. That the novel is prefaced with Nietzsche's maxim "What is done out of love always takes place beyond good and evil" gives sanction to the potential communion of love between Shar and Karen. The corollary is that what is done out of a violation of love is pernicious and life-denying. Like Grace of "Pastoral Blood," Karen is not comforted but embittered by the tenacious ties of family and place and by her recapitulation to a false Eden. She feels she has been denied a selfhood, that she has been initiated "into the communion of killers, murderers" (p. 221), the congregation of the faithful, who regularly sacrifice instinctual life to a dead god.

Shar's death also effects a "mock communion" (p. 183) for the Cherry River spectators at the race. His violent self-realization is reminiscent of Nietzsche's description of the Dionysian death throes at the heart of tragedy. Shar's earnest wish to penetrate through the "barrier" that separates himself from the rest of the world is equivalent to the tragic hero's "joyous hope that the spell of individuation may be broken in an augury of restored oneness."[6] Before his final race, Shar conjectures that the attraction of the race for the spectators is a vicarious courting of death and violence, "to force themselves into the men who represented them down on the track: they thirsted for death, they were fascinated by it, and envious of it" (p. 183). But although the sports arena functions like a theater, the spectators cannot truly participate in the tragic drama. Cut off from the action, they are denied a catharsis, left "pale and hysterical." In this particular race the spectators misconstrue the action, missing entirely Shar's tragic realization and his violent liberation into selfhood. Rather they search for a scapegoat upon which to blame the death, venting their destructive vengeance upon the black man who won the race, a vengeance that spreads out to include all blacks as a violent race riot ensues. This Dionysian fury is not a celebration but a destructive release of intolerable emotional tension. The Cherry River residents remain locked in their vulgar world of cheap commercialism, grotesque entertainment, and vicarious thrills. Oates's fascination with communal violence continues when in a subsequent novel, *them*, she depicts the 1967 Detroit riot, but the joyous awakening to instinctual life portrayed there is not matched by a similar liberation here, where insidious racial hatred is unleashed upon an innocent enemy.

Like so much of Oates's work, *With Shuddering Fall* at first appears to be written merely for the best-seller market, centering as it does on the tumultuous life and love of a racetrack driver. But although it is indeed full of those perennial best-seller ingredients—sex and violence—they are here neither gratuitous nor sensationally used. Superimposed upon the unlikely racetrack context is a dense and difficult network of literary and philosophical allusion, effected in part through Shar's promoter, the worldy-wise, overly civilized epicure who speculates about the childlike state of Shar and Karen. The novel reverberates with allusions to and echoes of the Bible and

Paradise Lost, Friedrich Nietzsche and Sören Kierkegaard, George Meredith and D. H. Lawrence. Some allusions are overt, others implicit; some conscious, some perhaps unconscious. Oates's acknowledged debt to other writers is especially apparent in this first novel where the thin characterization and action cannot always carry the heavy philosophical import attached to them. In Oates's later work, the synthesis is greater, the characters and action more fully realized in their own right. Indeed, perhaps the novel's most blatant weakness is the failure of the two main characters, Shar and Karen, to come to life as credible creations. Lacking reality, they do not engage the reader's empathy and sympathy. Nonetheless, *With Shuddering Fall* is a highly important part of Oates's apprenticeship, establishing as it does structural patterns, character types, and thematic concerns which will recur, almost formulaically, in her next five novels.

Just as this novel begins with an explosive scene of family and sexual violence—the bloody confrontation between Shar and Mr. Herz and the ensuing sexual liaison between the lovers—so too does each of the next five novels contain such a scene. Just as Shar seeks liberation from the constrictions of an anonymous and isolated self, so too will each succeeding novel portray the quest of the central male character. Just as Karen is locked in a selfless void, so Oates's future female characters will also be. Just as the central action here focuses on the powerful magnetism between a man and a woman which pulls them back and forth between the bonds of home and freedom, between the potential liberation of love and of violence, so too will most of the subsequent novels be focused. Here, in short, Oates has sketched some of the most basic concerns which continue to haunt her for a number of years. The later novels offer more satisfactory treatment of these concerns because of their fuller realization of character and scene and the more skillful integration of rhetorical points into the action. But this novel will continue to be important for the patterns it can be seen to establish for Oates's later fiction.

CHAPTER 3

The Trilogy of Social Groups: The Quest for Violent Liberation

A Garden of Earthly Delights, Expensive People, and *them,* although in many ways dissimilar, form a trilogy sharing structural and thematic similarities. Each novel depicts a family from an American social group: the Walpoles of *A Garden* are migrant workers; the Everetts of *Expensive People,* affluent suburbanites; the Wendalls of *them,* urban poor. Each novel concentrates upon the repercussions of the family's life-style upon the psychological development of its children. Oates claims that the three novels "are put together in parallel construction. Each deals with a male imagination and consciousness that seeks to liberate itself from certain confinements."[1] The central male characters, Swan Walpole, Richard Everett, and Jules Wendall—like the prototype before them, Shar Rule—are all obsessed with breaking out of intolerable confinements objectified in a cohesive parent-child bond, and each resorts to violence. Swan attempts to kill his mother but inadvertently kills his "father" and deliberately kills himself. Similarly, Richard kills his mother (at least, ostensibly) and plans to kill himself. Only in the final novel of the trilogy, *them,* does the central male character, Jules, successfully complete his quest for liberation. Like Shar—but unlike the two others—his anger, resentment, and rebellion are directed not against the mother, but against the father, against constricting authoritarian structures. When he kills a father-surrogate, a policeman, he frees himself from his father's crushing defeat by the environment. Like Shar blazing to selfhood in his death, Jules rediscovers his instinctual being. The quest for liberation of the self is the very heart of Oates's fiction, taking quite different form in each of the novels. Together, the three novels of this trilogy present a densely rich, probing dramatization of the quest.

48

I   A Garden of Earthly Delights: *Naturalistic Allegory*

A Garden of Earthly Delights naturalistically depicts the crippling psychological effects engendered first by the economic and social deprivation of migrant workers and then by the displacements and adjustments accompanying the changing position in society of successive generations. Oates's focus upon the shaping influence of environment upon character development is intensified by sectioning the novel into three parts, each focusing on a male character— Carleton, Lowry, and Swan—who is arrested at a different stage by social and psychological barriers. Allegorically, the novel depicts the quest by these three men to return to the lost Garden of Eden and to be reconciled with the stern but just and orderly world of the Father.

The vehicle of explusion from the Garden was initially the Great Depression. In part one, Carleton, whose parental family was uprooted by the Depression, lives alienated and isolated from the migrant life in which he finds himself caught. Eager to maintain the intellectual and temperamental differences between himself and the others, he is yet unable to break out of the vicious cycle of his life, unable to stop the endless pregnancies and the creeping insanity of his wife, and unable to establish himself in the dominant culture with a permanent job in a settled location. Carleton longs for his dead father and the life he had known before inexplicable events sent him upon the endless treadmill of the migrant worker. He wishes to recapture the lost past or at the very least to establish a meaningful connection to it. His daughter Clara reminds him of his young wife; she seems to erase the ravages of time, seems to give him a chance to start again. But his daughter runs away, and he dies without locating her and without making that important connection between the past and present.

In part two, Lowry, a young man in his mid-twenties who befriends Clara when she is a young teenager, is nearly a mirror image of Carleton as Oates invites the reader to view his life as a variant of the same oppressive pattern of displacement and alienation. His family were impoverished hired workers, but unlike Carleton, he broke out of their depressing syndrome by severing all bonds to this group; his discerning, restless intellect, in fact, makes him dissatisfied with even an ordinary life-style. He seeks the Garden in the world of thought and experience beyond the narrow confines of his impoverished life. After rescuing Clara, a slightly dirty, common, and cheap young girl, from the migrant-worker life, setting her up with a job and a room in a little country town and unknowingly impregnating her, he suddenly leaves. While away for a number of years, he marries a wife to whom he can talk, but he grows tired, unable to talk out his permanent malaise. Divorced by his wife, he travels around Europe, joins the army, and gets injured in the war. Finally, he is drawn back inexorably to Clara. But she, rejected before by him, now in turn rejects him for the opportunity she sees to become the wife of Revere, the affluent farmer and businessman who cares for her and her child. Lowry drifts out of the novel into, most probably, a life of permanent displacement excluded forever from realized selfhood and from any Garden of Earthly Delights.

In part three, Swan, Clara and Lowry's child who shares the blond good looks of his father and grandfather, is at yet a further stage along the social scale, further removed from the cycle of economic and social deprivation of the migrant workers. Although he is initially an illegitimate child, Revere eventually marries his mother; and he is taken in as the son Revere supposed him to be. While Clara basks in the wealth and position of the Revere family, thinking that she and her son have successfully established themselves in the Garden of Earthly Delights, Swan is plagued with insecurity, alienation, and—importantly—guilt. He feels guilt for the strange father, Lowry, who once visited his mother and must be forever hidden from Revere, and he tries to win acceptance from Revere as a son and as a brother to his three sons. Like Karen Herz in *With Shuddering Fall*, he also is fascinated by the Old Testament God of Bible readings, and ultimately he seeks the cleansing punishment of this transcendent Father.

While Carleton felt painfully the expulsion from the Garden and Lowry sought unsuccessfully to replace the lost innocence of Eden with a full embrace of consciousness and experience, neither felt personally guilty or responsible for his failure. But Swan feels guilty about his impending success. As the illegitimate son of a daughter of migrant workers, who was to snatch the wealth and position of Revere from the hands of his heirs, Swan was to be the beautiful bird to emerge from the ugly duckling. Why is he unable to assume the position so esteemed by his mother and so envied by his disenfranchised father and grandfather? He has the intelligence and ability; he knows the managerial details of Revere's estate better than the man does himself. But he is unable to overcome his guilt. The "wings" with which he was to soar over the Reveres are instead beating inside his head, driving him to the desperate destructive relief he takes: "In his brain there was a bird fluttering to get out. He was aware of it in his most helpless, frantic moments, or when he was exhausted. Its wings beat against the walls of his head, pounding along with his pounding ears, and would not give him peace" (p. 308).[2] Psychologically, he is no more able to break into the world of the Reveres than Carleton and Lowry were. He has been maimed by his insecurity and by his mother's driving ambition and like Karen Herz, he feels compelled to act out a prescribed role dictated by a parent. Here it is the mother rather than the father who circumscribes his free will and predetermines his destiny as a killer.

As a young child Swan is told by Lowry that it would be his destiny to kill many things. The boy feels the need to be a hunter to win the approval of Revere, but he is repelled by the thought of killing. Yet he is responsible for the accidental death of his stepbrother, Robert, since he angrily pushed him when returning from an abortive hunting trip, causing Robert's gun to go off. In fact, he feels that he and his mother bring nothing but destruction and disorder to the Revere family. His mother callously encourages the eldest son Clark's dissipation and involvement with disreputable women, because it lessens the likelihood that he will be taken in as a partner in his father's business. She even goes so far as to flirt casually with him so that in a moment of drunken release of inhibition, Clark makes a pass at her. The next day she uses this indiscretion to call for his removal from the house and encourages him to marry a girl of whom Revere does not approve. Jonathan, the son who had always been regarded as intelligent and spirited, becomes increasingly morose and backward after Swan's admission into the household, because Swan's intelligence apparently so dwarfs his own.

Finally, Swan, longing for identification with a transcendent Father of moral justice and an earthly father of love, feels driven to right the wrongs he and his mother have inflicted upon the Revere family. But even this murderous act turns out to be wrongly destructive. He kills the very person, Revere, for whom he had attempted to make things right; and his incorrigible mother escapes his avenging gun, although the extinction of all her hopes and dreams does break her sanity, and she spends the rest of her long life in a mental institution.

A Garden of Earthly Delights, like *With Shuddering Fall*, explores the nature of innocence. Also like Oates's first novel, it is dependent upon allusion to complete its thematic statement, only the referent now is in art rather than literature and philosophy. As Rose Marie

Burwell has demonstrated,[3] the title of the novel probably alludes to Hieronymous Bosch's medieval painting—often called *The Garden of Earthly Delights*. Since Oates is inviting the reader to see parallels between the triptych's panels and the tripartite novel, the naturalism of the novel is moderated by the moral implications of the painting. Just as Bosch's painting is interpreted as "a didactic treatment of the fate of mankind—in Eden disobedient, in the earthly garden sinful, in hell expiating the deeds of sinful lives" so too can Oates's novel be construed as a moral fable, so that what has been interpreted as a melodramatic climax—Swan's attempted murder of his mother resulting in the deaths of Revere and himself—can be more satisfactorily seen as the inevitable working out of the moral pattern. The final brief chapter depicting Clara in a mental institution is the equivalent of Bosch's hell scene. Burwell has pointed out parallels to Bosch; I wish here to look at the implications of this moral pattern upon characterization.

The guilt Swan feels is as real as that experienced by Henry Sutpen in William Faulkner's *Absalom, Absalom!*, a similar across-the-generation study in innocence and guilt. Both sons have inherited rather than personally initiated the moral wrong. Clara, like Thomas Sutpen, is innocently evil, a condition particularly pernicious and particularly American. Like the child Sutpen who came down from an equalitarian community in the hills to learn discrimination and privilege, Clara as a young girl quickly learns that migrant workers are considered less human than others, that they have a way of speaking, acting, and looking which distinguishes them as pariahs from their fellow human beings. Like Sutpen, she is determined to overcome these differences by assimilating into and triumphing over the dominant culture. Some of the most effective passages of the novel depict Clara's pathetic attempts at self-improvement: her painted orange-crate dressers, her garishly pink dime-store rug, her decorative nature pictures, and her kitten-cute calendar. Lowry winces at her efforts and at her imitative and painstaking grooming which achieve either ludicrous or cheap and common results. But Clara is determined to succeed, and even when Lowry is chiding her for her incorrigible commonness, she is imitating his speech patterns, trying to erase her telltale accent and dialect.

She falls keenly in love with Lowry, but he is unable to commit himself to her, determined as he is to sever all bonds with his former life. When she discovers that she is pregnant, she realizes that she must take her life in hand. She becomes a self-directed person shaped by choices, not by accident: "The day Clara took her life into control was an ordinary day. She did not know up until the last moment exactly how she would bring all those accidents into control. . . . All her life she would be able to say: Today she changed the way her life was going and it was no accident. No accident" (pp. 189, 198). At this point of conscious control Clara initiates the pattern of moral culpability which eventually engulfs her son and herself. She is, like Karen Herz of *With Shuddering Fall*, deliberately closing herself off from her lover's passion and seeking instead to "win" through mastery and control. Capitalizing on Revere's interest in her, she leads him into a sexual encounter and then lets him believe that he is the father of her child. He provides for her as a mistress for a number of years and then, when his wife dies, he marries her. Clara had calculated and planned for these developments, just as she plots her son's triumph over Revere's sons. She has grown from the delicate and naive girl who relied on strong men to care for her to an opportunistic and hard woman. Whereas Karen Herz can never free herself from her dependency upon her father, from her need to borrow her strength from a source outside of herself, and thus can never overcome her own vacuousness, Clara—after breaking from both her father and her fatherlike lover, Lowry—takes her own life in hand. But this control is a narrowing rather than a blooming of the self. It is concomitant with a deadening of the emotional life, a closing off to the potentialities of love. Where Karen's nullity will be portrayed again in subsequent Oatesian women—in Maureen and Nadine of *them*, Elena of *Do With Me What You Will*, Helene of *Wonderland*, Yvonne of *The Assassins*, and Laney of *Childwold*—Clara shares a sisterhood with a different group of women—Loretta of *them*, Nada of *Expensive People*, Ardis of *Do With Me What You Will*, Arlene of *Childwold*, among others. Having perfected the art of survival, these women are supremely egotistical. Although Clara claims to have done it all for Swan, he knows that she is deceiving herself, that she cares only about herself.

While Oates usually neither idealizes nor condemns these strong female figures, *A Garden* provides a moral and allegorical frame of reference absent in the other novels. Clara, for all her "innocence," acts as an evil force in this Eden County Garden of Earthly Delights, and she lives a subsequent life in hell—the mental hospital—in payment for her transgressions. To be sure, she never gains any insight into herself and her moral culpability. Oates, in fact, by so vividly portraying the prominent role of environmental influences in shaping character, sympathetically dramatizes Clara's predicament.

Oates here faces this problem of moral accountability versus moral naiveté in the same way that William Faulkner does in *Absalom, Absalom!* She demonstrates that evil is inherently self-destructive. "Evil" for both writers is a calculated self-interest with which one deliberately closes off feeling, passion, and compassion. Oates, like Faulkner, Lawrence, and Nietzsche, is unable to characterize sexual love as evil. Rather "what is done out of love always takes place beyond good and evil." Sexual love is man responding to the natural emotional and biological drives within himself, man seeking to transcend the limitations of his individual selfhood. An explicit denial of feelings and a deliberate aborting of love is irreparably destructive in Oates's world. First Lowry and then Clara place plans for self-betterment ahead of the natural development of their relationship, and so they are each responsible for the failure of their potentially liberating love. They fail to value their relationship because a discriminatory society makes each feel a necessity to be separated from a pattern of failure, to latch on to someone who is undeniably secure in the dominant culture. Oates, like Faulkner, does not suggest that her characters could have been different; it is Swan who more clearly sees the blame and suffers the guilt for the devastation that Clara brings to the Revere family. Like many of Faulkner's characters—particularly Charles Bon and Henry Sutpen—Swan feels he must act out a role in a drama larger than that provided by his individual selfhood, a role which denies him free will.

Clara's innocently evil actions, then—given the morally accountable universe that Oates constructs in *A Garden*—are inimical to life and thus inherently self-destructive. Just as Thomas Sutpen's design crumbles around him as members of his family literally kill off one another in Faulkner's *Absalom, Absalom!*, so too does Clara's "design" destroy itself from within as her supposedly triumphant son fires his murderous gun. Yet in spite of the moral or poetic justice of Swan's actions, Clara's resultant madness is surprising. The quality that these strong female figures share as Oates characterizes them is their adjustability: Loretta, Nada, and Ardis do not fall apart when faced with crises. Similarly, Clara is the epitome of stability: "Clara . . . had always been at the center of herself, whether she was nine or eighteen or twenty-eight, as she was now. Whatever else happened, that Clara never changed" (p. 289). She has weathered the radical displacements and catastrophes of her life. She is, for example, the strong-stomached individual who kept her wits and rushed Robert to the hospital after the bloody hunting accident. Never showing any signs of mental instability, she is, in my opinion, unlikely to fall apart even at the violent deaths of her husband and son.

Where Karen Herz's mental breakdown is a natural outgrowth of a lifetime of instability, the final chapter depicting Clara in a mental hospital lacks credibility, perhaps because the heavy-handed imposition of the moral pattern of Bosch's painting upon the book jars with Oates's usual skepticism. The destruction of Clara's sanity with a single stroke of poetic justice is unconvincing. Joyce Carol Oates's fictional world is typically peopled with two kinds of human beings, those who have adjusted and those who have not. Usually those who have adjusted do so because of their ratlike limitations, while those who are most sensitive and intelligent are almost invariably too weak to overcome debilitating sociological and psychological conditioning. In this novel Oates has for the most part successfully combined a naturalistic portrayal of the descendants of migrant workers with a moral fable of evil's inherent self-destructiveness, but in so doing she has infused her work with a sense of transcendent moral justice working itself in human affairs which is quite at odds with the objective, skeptical naturalism of the bulk of her fiction.

II   Expensive People: *Satire of Literary and Suburban Conventions*

The first-person narrator of *Expensive People*, Richard Everett, shocks the reader by his initial statement, "I was a child murderer" (p. 5).[4] The novel is a "memoir" of this precocious eighteen-year-old who attempts to explain to the reader and to himself why he murdered his mother, Nada. His father, Elwood Everett, is a highly successful corporate executive; his mother, Nada, a successful novelist whose life is schizophrenically divided between desperate conformity to suburban life-style and bohemian rebellion against it. Sporadically, she is ferociously ambitious for and protective of her son. But she is also restless and selfish, pursuing affairs with lovers and taking off from home for long periods. Indeed, the immediate cause of Richard's alleged matricide is his despair when he perceives that she is going to leave home once again. Richard's claim to matricide, however, like all the other "facts" he relates, is open to grave doubt.

While one *could* explain the anomalous facts discrediting Richard's claim that he murdered his mother (the buried gun may have been stolen or removed; his attendance at school easily faked or erroneously recorded), yet the reader has other reasons to question Richard's credibility, since he has all the bias of a highly subjective first-person narrator. He admits that like his mother he has problems distinguishing the real and the fictional in his own life: "I think my problems about life, about what is real and what is fiction in my own life, in this memoir, might come from her, though I don't want to blame her for anything" (p. 53). Also like her he believes that "what was 'only real' couldn't be very important" (p. 85). He regularly fictionalizes himself for his parents, making up stories about boys at school (p. 71), imitating the person his mother thinks he is (p. 187), playing at being healthy (p. 195). Furthermore, the seemingly real is often fictional: humorously interspersed in the narrative are two vividly credible television rehearsals, the first a bank robbery and murder, which may have planted the idea of murder—real or make-believe—in Richard's mind ("I had never seen anyone killed in front of me, even if it did turn out to be make-believe" [p. 75]); the second, a spectacular accident on the freeway (p. 132). Moreover, Richard inadvertently acts out a fiction, one of his mother's sketches for a story to be called "The Sniper" (p. 117), when he plays the role of sniper and murderer. When his dog Spark is run over and killed, his parents fabricate fictions ("Spark needs his measles shot") and substitute another dog the next day. When the second dog is also killed, they do it again, only now the dog is bigger and not so soft and friendly (pp. 145-48). In a world where make-believe deaths seem real and real deaths are denied, the "truth" about Nada's death is problematical.

Ultimately, of course, it doesn't matter whether the murder is real or delusional; Richard's disturbances are "real" and his complex feelings about his mother are the same. While his morose suffering is potentially a serious and painful subject, it doesn't engage the reader's concern, however, for Richard is an overdrawn caricature, like all the other characters in the novel. This tour-de-force is an anomaly in Oates's canon. Rather than a piece of naturalistic realism like her other novels, it is a masterful satire of both literary and suburban conventions. At the core of the novel is Oates's questioning—at once playful and probing—of the elusive nature of both life and art.

Richard, like innumerable first-person narrators before him, insists upon the veracity of his narrative. His "memoir" "isn't well rounded or hemmed in by fate in the shape of novelistic architecture. It certainly isn't well planned. It has no conclusion but just dribbles off, in the same way that it begins. This is life" (p. 6) The sine qua non of the novel that Oates mocks here is, as Ian Watt has explained, "formal realism"—"the premise, or primary convention, that the novel is a full and authentic report of human experience."[5] Yet Richard knows that the very process of attempting to report his "real" experience falsifies it. He experiments with possible openings, knowing full well that each rendition will create a different "story" and that none will satisfactorily translate his inchoate feelings into "meaning" or "truth":

My problem is that I don't know what I am doing. I lived all this mess but I don't know what it is. I don't even know what I mean by "it." I have a story to tell, yes, and no one else could tell it but me, but if I tell it now or next year it will come out one way, and if I could have forced my fat, heaving body to begin this a year ago it would have been a different story then. And it's possible that I'm lying without knowing it. Or telling the truth in some weird, symbolic way without knowing it, so only a few psychoanalytic literary critics (there are no more than three thousand) will have access to truth, what "it" is. (p. 7)

But Richard establishes a very cozy and conversational relationship with the reader: "One morning in January a yellow Cadillac pulled up to a curb. And let's freeze that scene so I can sketch it all in. You see the Cadillac? Good. See if you can smell its new leathery odor" (p. 10). He is conscious of his role as scene-maker and, in spite of his alleged attempt merely to record his "memoir," he is also attempting to do it right, to make it "art." Richard's search in Chapter Two for historical and literary precedents, for example, is Oates's burlesquing of literary scholarship, for Richard dredges up unlikely parallels. He isolates several either apocryphal or ludicrously strained accounts of youthful murderers, one of the more ridiculous being "the allusion in *Macbeth* to Lady Macbeth, as a child, wantonly doing away with a 'blessed babe,' no doubt a sibling" (p. 9).[6] He acknowledges some literary precursors, and one is reminded of others. For example, he suggests that Herman Melville is a model for his symbolism and for the method and tricks he uses to heighten the significance of his tale: "Therefore you will allow me certain rhetorical flourishes and tricks, and the pathetic Melvillian device of enormous build-ups for flabby walk-ons—opening paragraphs and even entire chapters that pave the way concretely enough while frisking about on a kind of ethereal abstract level in order to relate my confession to things sublime and infinite" (p. 90). Obviously there is a great deal of self-parody in

Richard's description; his citation of Melville is less significant than his mockery of himself. Through his self-consciousness about his writing, Oates underscores the inevitable artificiality and imitativeness of literature. Richard simply wants to tell his true story, but he is troubled by the falseness that creeps into his tale when he attempts to transcribe it into words and to invest it with meaning. For example, a footnote to Chapter Eight, part one, reads: "As I read this over, this rendition of infant impressions strikes me very bad, but let it stand. The experince is there, the reality is there, but how to get at it? Everything I type out turns into a lie simply because it is not the truth" (p. 31). The sandwiching of theoretical chapters on the art of writing within the narrative is more reminiscent of Henry Fielding's *Tom Jones* than it is of *Moby Dick*, just as Richard's articulate ennui recalls Dowell's in Ford Madox Ford's *The Good Soldier*. The latter parallel is especially noticeable when Richard, like Dowell, engages in maudlin self-pity, when he notes that his perception of his story changes with the passing of time, and when he confesses, as Dowell repeatedly does, that he simply cannot make sense out of what has happened to him.

Moreover, Richard also calls into question the origin of art which doesn't grow out of lofty inspiration and according to rules of beauty and order; rather, "of all human endeavors 'art' is the most pulsating, rippling, seething, improbable, and unpredictable of all the creations of man. . . . It's all as Tennyson remarked wisely, 'We poets are vessels to produce poetry and other excrement' " (p. 87). Because of this discussion of the base and disorderly origin of literary inspiration, Oates's parody of the formulaic rules of creative-writing handbooks and magazine articles is especially humorous. Richard has consulted such resources as well as literary classics as models for his work and his cataloguing of the rules they have provided him is ludicrously reductive:

4. I provide some possibility—don't I? for "reader identification." (My theory is that we have all been children, each of us. I hope this common experience is enough.)

5. I provide a moral stance. (Indeed I do, and this stance I am taking with poor, blistered, sweating, swollen feet flat on the earth is that crime does not pay. It is not very original, I know.)

6. I write in a clear story line, with specific illustrations and description

limited to "what's really necessary," (See January 1967, *Amateur Penman,* "Just What is Really Necessary in Your Writing?") (p.89)

Oates even slyly parodies herself, as Richard consults one of her published articles entitled "Building Tension in a Short Story': "I have based some of them [chapters] on an article concerned with 'building suspense' and—you see how honest I am—even dull stretches can be used to build suspense if there is the promise of some violence to come" (p. 88).

As Richard imagines reviews of his books, Oates delights in mocking parodies of the styles of the *New York Times Book Review, Time, New Republic,* and a literary quarterly. For example, the punning, too-clever, superficial response of the reviewer of *Time* is matched by the dense, sociological pondering of the *New Republic's*:

Everett sets out to prove that he can outsmart Sartre but doesn't quite make it. It is great fun though. As there should be, there are Problems with Mother. But these are probably resolved as the novel progresses. Hijinks galore, but, like a damp firecracker, most of them smolder rather than explode. (p. 134)

Expensive People has as its verbal mode the reduction of a generation's anguish to the insufferable lyricism of one child; as the talisman of at least one plane of its purported operations, it exhibits vast mountains of junk (middle-class acquistions, symbolic of life), about which its child-narrator turns dizzily, dreaming not simply the manic dream of the middle class (which never wakes in this novel), but also the manic dream of the would-be novelist who would reduce complex sociological material to a thalamic crisis. (p. 134)

(Amusingly, the actual review of the novel in *Time* bears a distinct tonal and stylistic resemblance to Oates's parody.[7]) Richard shows himself to be a perceptive critic of one of his mother's stories, "The Molesters," included in the volume, as the story in turn attests to Nada's talent as a writer. The story is an example of how life— Richard's relationship with his mother—is transformed into fiction. But since the story is in fact one of Oates's own previously published stories, it also breaks down the borders between the real author, Joyce Carol Oates, and the fictional one, Nada, inviting us to look for parallels.

Not only is fiction, then, based on the real, reality is often fictionalized and unreal, especially the world of stultifying sameness and sterility that is upper-middle-class suburbia. The interchangeable suburban communities that the family moves through on Elwood Everett's corporate rise contain the same people, the same architecture and landscape, are located in the same place in relationship to the city, characterized by the same life-style, and governed by the same conventions and attitudes. In fact, a week after the Everetts move to Fernwood, they encounter a man whom they had known in Brookfield, who has also just moved, but absurdly they pretend not to know each other. Even the corporate circles are the same, and Nada's response reveals her terror of the claustrophobia of their world: "The bastard was just as terrified at seeing us as we were at seeing him. None of us can ever escape" (p. 28).

It is a world of ephemeral human relationships; indeed, Nada and Elwood are uncertain about whether one couple they wish to invite to a dinner party are alive or dead! It is a world where one has chipmunks rather than rats for house pests, agreeability rather than discord from house guests: "Everyone agreed with Mr. Body, even when they weren't listening. Everyone agrees with everyone else in Fernwood, or Cedar Grove, whereever we are" (p. 198). One of Nada's intellectual friends who lectures to a group of her suburban friends blurts out:

"I am, frankly, amazed at the artificiality of this suburban world. Your very children look artificial, do you realize that? Type-cast, healthy, well-fed, tanned children with no cares, no problems, no duties, no responsibilities, no sufferings, no thoughts, children out of a Walt Disney musical! And these children are your products, my friends. Think of what you are creating!" . . .
"That's fascinating," a woman said. "Is it tied in with your work?" (p. 200)

(But Oates can cut both ways: this intellectual, it turns out, cherishes as the most significant happening of his life, his introduction to Princess Margaret!)

It is a world of conspicuous luxury and affluence: "mixed in with the odor of lawns being sprinkled automatically on warm spring mornings is the odor of money, cash. Fresh, crisp cash. Bills you could stuff in your mouth and chew away at" (p. 33). It is an efficient, well-run world dependent upon countless paid services to keep it that way. In one of the most amusing passages, Nada, on the day of their arrival in yet another suburb, Cedar Grove, makes a series of telephone calls on her plastic princess phone, setting the vast service mechanism into order. These calls include: Cedar Grove Employment Services for domestic help; Cedar Grove Plumbing; Cedar Grove Green Carpet Lawn Services for "mowing, fertilizing, shrub and tree spraying, weed and insect spraying. . . . Yes, fungus prevention, everything, edging, thinning, rolling, flattening. The usual. Everything" (p. 155); the Gas Company; the Badger Insurance Company; Cedar Grove Garbage Disposal Service; the Sanitation Department; Good Will; Cedar Grove Junior High School; Cedar Grove Bank of the Commonwealth; Cedar Grove Eye Clinic; Roman Wall, a restaurant; the Electric Company; the Water Company; the Telephone Company; Cedar Grove House of Beauty; Cedar Grove Key Makers; and the Continental Market Basket for home deliveries of groceries and delicacies. Miraculously, these calls are all successful and Nada leans back in pretended exhaustion over the execution of her wifely duties.

It is a world that Nada had wanted desperately. Like F. Scott Fitzgerald's Gatsby, she covers up her mundane origins with fictionalized romantic tales and like him she propels herself into the glittering life of the rich and holds on to it tenaciously. But like Fitzgerald, her attitude to the affluent life she has craved is riddled with disdain and ambivalence. Dedicated to the craft of writing and gifted with apparently genuine talent, she yet underplays her "real" identity as a writer, thinking it will diminish her acceptance as an equal in the community. Rather, she deliberately puts on the fabricated image and style of the suburban matron, playing the roles of a status-seeking, country-clubbing socialite and of a concerned and eager mother who frets over her child's enrollment in the most prestigious and snobbish English-style private school. But paradoxically the "real" Nada—the bohemian free spirit, the intelligent, sensual, gifted woman—emerges, and periodically she abandons her family, leaving her son Richard shaken and dismayed.

Nada is reminiscent of Clara in *A Garden* with her determined social climbing, but unlike her, she is implausible and unsympathetic as a character—not because such a woman could not exist, but because she is portrayed only from the outside. She is seen only from Richard's perspective, and his account is colored with the mockery, hurt, and excessive love of a rejected child. Nada is shown at her worst, from an ironic distance, and the reader has little chance to empathize with that "other" Nada as the credible self whose restlessness and suffering are genuine. "Nada" is more easily seen as the emblem of the nothingness idolized in this materialistic suburban world. The stifling of her individuality is more deliberate but no worse really that the stifling of the other standardized inhabitants of this affluent desert.

Richard's alleged matricide is in part a gesture against his mother and the empty world she has chosen, but it has further ramifications. Although this novel is radically different in execution and tone from Oates's other novels, it is typical in its focus upon a violent response to a cohesive familial bond. Indeed, Richard's quest for liberation—like Swan's in *A Garden*—takes murderous expression. His killing of his mother parallels Swan's attempt to kill his. But neither son is freed through violence from his unhealthy bondage to his mother, and Richard intends to duplicate Swan's suicide. He attempts to console himself with the belief that "whatever I did, whatever degradations and evils, stupidities, blunders, moronic intrusions, whatever single ghastly act I did manage to achieve, it was done out of freedom, out of choice. This is the only consolation I have in the face of my death, my readers: the thought of my free will" (pp. 255–56). But incapable of a "free" and spontaneous act, he is deceiving himself, as he indeed suspects: "But I must confess that there are moments when I doubt even this consolation." Perhaps Richard vaguely recollects, as certainly the reader does, that he has acted out his mother's sketch "The Sniper." His psychiatrist does not believe that he actually killed his mother, but he does accurately describe Richard's motivation: his excessive love for his mother caused him to want to be his mother's destroyer and thereby "establish forever a relationship between the two of us which no one could transcend, not even my father" (p. 253). In other words, his violent act was less an attempt to "free" himself from his bondage to his mother than it was to "fix" forever inviolable the Oedipal relationship. But Richard feels cheated out of the effectiveness of his act, because no one believes that he did it. He does not receive the punishment that he needs; consequently, he tries to perpetuate this act of violence by the writing of his memoir: "a hatchet to slash through my own heavy flesh and through the flesh of anyone else who happens to get in the way" (p. 6). But the act of writing is merely a prelude to his planned suicide. Meanwhile, like so many of Oates's characters, he regresses to an infantile mode where excessive eating substitutes inadequately for the lack of maternal nurturance.

Nonetheless, the dispassionate reader is unable to shed a tear over Richard's plight. Swan's misery in *A Garden* is much more painful. Although *Expensive People*, like *A Garden*, is a portrayal of the repercussions of an American family's life-style upon its child, this account of affluent suburbia is markedly different. Oates's satirical bias colors and distances the view. Similarly, the self-consciousness of Richard's narration—accompanied as it is by Oates's playful parodies of literary styles, rules, and conventions—adds to this distance. Richard and the other characters fail to become convincingly realistic. But the novel succeeds in different terms and in those it should be judged. Oates misleadingly invites us to parallel *Expensive People* with *A Garden* and *them;* but in spite of some similarities, the differences are enormous. Unique among her novels, *Expensive People* is Oates's successful experiment with the satirical mode.

III   them: *Parody of Naturalism*

Focusing on the plight of the urban poor, *them*, the third novel of the trilogy, counterpoints the lives of two central characters—Jules and Maureen, brother and sister—who respond to their shared familial environment in radically different ways. Both are "Children of Silence" (p. 7)[8] oppressed by the angry, silent father, Howard Wendall, who is finally crushed to death in an accident in a Detroit factory, a death graphically in keeping with the psychic maiming that has been his life. He has been incapable of any degree of self-definition or understanding. The weak son of a domineering mother, Howard "saves" Loretta, a young girl, by disposing of the body of her dead lover—murdered gratuitously by her brother Brock—and then marrying her. He progresses on a steady course downward on the social scale from crooked cop to factory worker and inward into frustrated and angry silence. Jules and Maureen fear and hate their father. Jules, in fact, in Oedipal fashion, imagines that he kills him (p. 88). The weak father figure is just one of the many deprivations of their impoverished rearing.

Loretta, their mother, garrulously fills the void of her husband's teeming silence. This self-centered, often foul-mouthed woman adapts more successfully to their downward slump and maintains some semblance of identity. The girl who lovingly contemplated her image in the mirror, who dressed and acted in the exact style of the age, and who waited with anticipation for "what would happen," becomes a hardened, dowdy, middle-aged woman. But Loretta's strength, like Clara's in *A Garden*, is her adaptability. Like the rats, she finds a home in the slums. With her bouncy walk and her incessant talk, Loretta maintains a healthy self-esteem, in spite of the potentially traumatizing events of her life. But Loretta is too self-centered, too acclimatized to the slums, too insensitive to serve as an effective parental guide for Jules and Maureen.

Maureen attempts to be a good student and obedient daughter, whereas Jules takes to the streets young, committing minor theft first, then embarking by chance on an abortive career as driver for an underworld figure, Bernard Geffen. Falling in love on sight with a highly neurotic rich girl, Nadine Greene, he runs off with her to Texas. She deserts him after a few days, and he drifts around the country for awhile, picking up odd jobs. After he has been back in Detroit for some years and is working for his uncle, a successful businessman, he encounters Nadine and they get involved again, until Nadine pulls out a gun and attempts to kill Jules and herself. Meanwhile Maureen has found out that she, too, must break out of the life in which she is caught. She resorts to prostitution to provide the money that seems to be necessary to effect her escape, but when she is discovered by her stepfather, Furlong, and severely beaten, she lapses into a vegetative state.

Just as Furlong's beating casts Maureen into extended catatonia, Nadine's shooting casts Jules into aimless drifting. Apathetic and lethargic, capable of only mindless sexual encounters, he becomes a peripheral member of the counterculture around Wayne State University. He even sinks to living off the earnings of a young girl whom he turns into a prostitute. But while Maureen gradually awakens out of her stupor and cautiously attempts to build up again the barriers around the self—this time by plotting a marriage to her college instructor who is married with three children and therefore safe and "pretested" as a husband—Jules is jolted out of his ennui by the Detroit riot. Jules participates directly in the riot by an act of violence: he murders a policeman.

At the end of the novel both characters have succeeded in getting out of the impoverished environment of their upbringing. Jules, who believes the Horatio Alger dream, is off to make his fortune in California, the golden land of American dreams. Similarly, his sister Maureen has achieved the dream of the American woman—a husband, a house in suburbia, and a baby on the way. Of course, these success stories are laden with irony. Jules is a punk, thief, pimp, and murderer before he opportunistically latches on to the antipoverty program which will finance his journey to California. Maureen's history of prostitution and her calculated husband-snatching similarly distance her from the "typical" American housewife.

On the face of it, *them* appears to be a naturalistic case study. It begins with an "Author's Note" which characterizes it as "a work of history in fictional form" based on the writer's experience as a teacher with a student at the University of Detroit and even includes, embedded in the narrative, two letters to "Joyce Carol Oates" from this student, "Maureen Wendall" (pp. 308–20). The alleged purpose of the note is to counter the reader's possible skepticism about the authenticity of the action: "Nothing in the novel has been exaggerated in order to increase the possibility of drama—indeed, the various sordid and shocking events of slum life, detailed in other naturalistic works, have been understated here, mainly because of my fear that too much reality would become unbearable." But in an interview Oates warned that this book is written in mock-naturalism, a form outdated and inappropriate to the material; that the note and the letters are totally fictitious, merely the trappings of a pseudonaturalistic report; and that one should not confuse the narrator with the author.[9] While Oates is probably crediting her audience with greater critical acumen than is warranted, since most readers failed to make this distinction, and since the "Joyce Carol Oates" of the prefatory note, in particular, is indistinguishable in any way from the "real" author; nonetheless, viewing the novel as a parody of a naturalistic novel makes for a much more satisfactory reading of it. Indeed, while a naturalistic novel characteristically records the defeat of the character by his environment, the two central characters in *them,* Jules and Maureen, succeed in getting out of their oppressed environment. As Oates has observed, reviewers and critics have underestimated the value of the sheer *survival* of her characters.

The novel demonstrates how far the poor are from the informing myths of our society and yet how compelling these myths are. The repetitive reference to the movies and television suggests that their lives are shaped by images from the media. Furthermore, there is a recurrent sameness to their lives, a disturbing replay of experiences in the lives of succeeding generations. One reviewer has observed these parallels and suggested that it negates individual differences among the characters: "all their lives are only random segments of a blind social continuum."[10] Despite similar appearances and experiences, however, the characters are not truly the same. Maureen is not Loretta; Brock is not Jules. Rather, the novel explores the nature of individual identity in a shared, oppressive environment. The main thrust of the novel is to contrast, not parallel, the lives of the two central characters. Out of the counterpointed stories of Jules and

Maureen arises the central thematic concern: how does one be one's self? In other words, what is selfhood in an environment seemingly so hostile to self-definition? Commentators have almost universally misunderstood Jules and the affirmative implications of his violent liberation.

As a young woman Loretta gathers strength from the conviction of her own unique selfhood which never totally leaves her: "There was a forlorn sensation in her, rising often, out of melancholy and weary joy, that everyone who was born must be a person—one person only—and that this personal, private, nameless kernel of the self could neither be broken down nor escaped from" (p. 56). Jules and Maureen share their mother's sense of the uniqueness of the self, but they have antithetical attitudes toward it, a polarity of attitude often depicted in Oates's male and female characters. To Maureen it is an intolerable burden, to Jules an inexplicable joy; to Maureen it means enclosure, to Jules freedom. "I only want to escape the doom of being *Maureen Wendall* all my life. I dream of a world where you can go in and out of bodies, changing your soul, everything changing and not fixed forever" (pp. 317–18). "Jules thought amiably, *Jules Wendall is my fate*, knowing it was not Nadine who shaped him but himself" (p. 277). Maureen's fearful retreat from life is apparent in her recurrent wish to join the toad that lives under the porch: "there was something in the very kinship between them, their similar breathlessness, their terror" (p. 129). Conversely, Jules is a "noisy, joyful child," "strangely independent," who "was not afraid of anyone" (p. 60). His affinity is with the spontaneous flames of fire: the burning wreck of a crashed plane and the fire he starts in the barn fascinate and transfix him as a child; the fires of the Detroit riot stir him to a new life as a young man. As a young girl Maureen entombs herself in the library, reading fiction by Jane Austen and others that seem more real than life, whereas Jules as a young boy opens himself to experience, making a self-created fiction out of his life: "he thought of himself as a character in a book being written by himself, a fictional fifteen-year-old with a capacity to become anything, because he was fiction. What couldn't he make out of himself?" (pp. 98–99). Maureen, incessantly cautious and fearful, is incapable of spontaneity: "Even when she played, even in her imagination she was somehow afraid of making a mistake" (p. 128). Jules is reckless and trusts in his instincts to determine the course of his life. Identifying with the American dream, he believes in his own infinite variety and infinite possibilities: "He could change his looks in five minutes. He could change himself to fit into anything" (p. 99). Maureen and Jules differ diametrically in their attitudes toward and feelings about other people. Jules seeks union with others; Maureen seeks protective isolation of the self. Jules is loving toward his mother and sisters; Maureen, in dark moments, "hated them all and wished they would die. She would like to shovel all their bodies under the veranda" (p. 120). Fascinated by an article by an Indian mystic which claimed that "we are all members of a single human family" (p. 95), Jules ponders the dilemma of the isolated self and the interconnected human family and articulates his thoughts, his love, and his longing in letters to his puzzled but proud mother: *"I am certain that there is Spirit of the Lord in us all, it makes us able to talk to one another and love one another"* (p. 306). The narrator underscores the "spiritual" nature of Jules's struggle for self-realization:

. . . were he writing his own story; his story would deal with the spirit exclusively. He thought of himself as pure spirit struggling to break free of the morass of the flesh. He thought of himself as spirit struggling with the fleshly earth, the very force of gravity, death. . . .

Of the effort the spirit makes, this is the subject of Jules's story; of its effort to achieve freedom, its breaking out into beauty, in patches perhaps but beauty anyway, and of Jules as an American youth—these are some of the struggles he would have thought worth recording. (p. 255)

Jules responds to his luck, his instincts, and his emotions as his truest self. His attractions to women are inexplicable but absolute, and he respects the intensity of his devotion. As a boy he takes to the fierce and spiritual Sister Jerome and to the neat and respectable Edith Kamensky. As a young man he falls in love on sight with Nadine. This attraction is in part a Gatsbylike infatuation with the oppressor class, but more importantly it is one of those promptings of "sensualized Platonism"[11] which Oates so values. Jules knows the dangers of pursuing a romance with this slightly mad rich girl, but he also knows that the intensity of the experience is worth the risk: "the essential Jules, the deeper, wiser, Jules, did no more than say constantly, *How could you live with yourself if you weren't equal to this—To this emotion?"* (p. 354).

Nadine is another Maureen, as in fact all of Jules's women are variants of "his other, darker self, his sister" (p. 248). Sister Jerome shares Maureen's repressed terror; Edith Kamensky, her compulsive orderliness; Nadine, her "melancholic frigidity." Jules's "desire for fusion, unity" (p. 373) is in a larger sense his quest for union with the obverse of himself: femaleness to his maleness, terror to his fearlessness, repression to his aggression, frigidity to his passion. Part of his unconscious attraction to women who are like his sister results from his need to identify with the totality of human experience, to commune with the "other darker self" within himself. Jules is occasionally cognizant of the similarities of Nadine and Maureen and of his shared inheritance of potential "madness": "At the height of his joy in this was a strange premonition of madness, his own madness or hers—the fear of madness, Maureen's blank stare, which might turn out to be his inheritance as well" (p. 268). He sees them both as similarly passive, frightened, and frigid recipients of sex and violence, unable to respond or escape: "like his sister Maureen, she was a woman who had to lie down to terror, submit to it, not having enough strength to escape" (p. 369).

Although they are at opposite ends of the social scale, Nadine and Maureen are mirror images of each other physically and emotionally; the dilemma of female identity knows no social class. Both are oppressed with the formlessness, the emptiness, of their lives which seem to consist of waiting for men to give them shape. In a letter, Maureen complains to Miss Oates, her English instructor:

Oh, we women know things you don't know, you teachers, you readers and writers of books, we are the ones who wait around libraries when it's time to leave, or sit drinking coffee alone in the kitchen; we make crazy plans for marriage but have no man, we dream of stealing men, we are the ones who look slowly around when we get off a bus and can't even find what we are looking for, can't quite remember how we got there, we are always wondering what will come next, what terrible thing will come next. We are the ones who leaf through magazines with colored pictures and spend long heavy hours sunk in our bodies, thinking, remembering, dreaming, waiting for something to come to us and give a shape to so much pain (p. 320).

Maureen wants to "arrange her life the way she arranged the kitchen after supper, and she too might then be frozen hard, fixed, permanent, beyond their ability to hurt" (p. 125). Similarly, Nadine claims, "I want to live a good, simple life. I want to put my faith in things that are simple and clear. That's all a woman asks. I want to put my life in order" (p. 350).

Maureen resorts to prostitution in an ill-fated attempt to achieve material security, but she never attempts sexual release. The cycles of a man's passion are to her nothing more than the cycles of a laundromat machine (p. 194). Only in her fantasies, never through her emotions, does Maureen find escape. She disassociates herself from the act of intercourse, even to the point of trying not to see the man's face (p. 190). She imagines riding away up North, as she sits placidly in the car of her "customer." Finally, when her prostitution is discovered and she is beaten nearly to death by her stepfather Furlong, her fantasy of a free self is even more extreme:

She is already on the bus, with her mother still gripping her, when she turns and sees her self step out of her body, with a sudden convulsive movement, freeing itself, escaping. This self is her. It steps down to the sidewalk again, pushing past other people who want to get on the bus. It glances back up at her. Everything rushes out of Maureen now and joins that other body, that free body, running away . . . it is like the terrible pressure of water wanting to burst free. How she yearns to join that body, get loose, scream with the pain and terror of getting loose. . . . (p. 206)

But the real Maureen, the inescapable selfless self, lies on the bed, a lump of flesh, whose voracious eating substitutes for unfulfilled psychic needs. Later, after she comes out of her stupor, she remains the same cautious, anxious, vacuous person she was before, only now she seeks to encase herself within the stereotypical role of American housewife: "Everything in me aches for a husband. A house" (p. 317). But her double, Nadine, has been unsuccessful at just such an attempt to achieve identity and fixity through marriage.

Because Nadine has experienced the ineffectuality of marriage in diminishing the terror of the void, her struggle is a stage beyond Maureen's. She tries to respond to the force of Jules's passion, tries to overcome her own frigidity. But unable to respond to the "fire" of his passion, she retreats to the "waters" of annihilation, the bathtub, as she had earlier during their trip to Texas contained her "sad, evil vision of purity" (p. 275) in the incessant washing of her hair. She would like to drown both of them (p. 368), yet ironically, she chooses Jules's own element, the fire of a gun, in an attempt to destroy them both.

After Nadine's shooting, Jules is no longer a joyful young man in pursuit of fusion and unity: "The spirit of the Lord departed from Jules" (p. 380). In fact, he becomes the equivalent of Maureen's seducer, procurer, and destroyer: beating one of his women, Vera, with a twisted coat hanger, he shares in his stepfather's brutality. But he is returned to himself through the riot: "Jules had not truly died but had only been slumbering, in an enchanted sleep; the spirit of the Lord had not truly departed from him" (p. 461). His lifelong fascination with fire is rekindled by the fires of the riot. He senses in the rioters the same responsiveness to instinctual feeling that he has trusted in and tried to be equal to: "Jules could see their joy. He felt touched by it, drawn to it. Let everything burn! Why not? The city was coming to life in fire, and he, Jules, was sitting in it, warming to it, the flames dancing along his arteries and behind his seared eyes" (pp. 459–60). Although the riot is destructive, it is also affirmative; it arises out of passion rather than repression, feeling rather than apathy.[12] Although it is difficult for some readers to accept his murderous act as an affirmative step toward selfhood, undoubtedly Oates wants us to see it that way. Oates herself observes that the hero's being a murderer is ironic,[13] but Jules, child of the ghetto, must act expediently. Earlier, when he was a kid, a policeman had chased and tried to kill him; now he gets his revenge. Furthermore, he must now kill the "father" (and not only is the policeman a "father figure," he bears an unmistakable resemblance to that other crooked cop, Howard Wendall) before he is similarly crushed and silenced by the constricting environment.

Later, when Jules comments enigmatically upon the riot during a television program, he quotes the Indian mystic whose article had inspired him as a boy: "fire burns and does its duty." He puzzles the other participants as he excitedly elaborates on his view:

"Violence can't be singled out from an ordinary day!" Jules cried. "Everyone must live through it again and again, there's no end to it, no land to get to, no clearing in the midst of the cities—who wants parks in the midst of the cities!—-parks won't burn." . . . "It won't hurt," his voice was saying earnestly. "The rapist and his victim rise up from the rubble, eventually, at dawn, and brush themselves off and go down the street to a diner. Believe me, passion can't endure! It will come back again and again but it can't endure!" (pp. 473–74)

Jules is attempting to articulate what the riot has helped to clarify: instability and impermanence are at the heart of human experience. Order, stability, permanence, unity are ephemeral goals: cities can burn; "violence can't be singled out from an ordinary day"; "passion can't endure"; nonetheless, this fluidity and unpredictability of human experience are no reason to despair, to give up. Rather, they are reason to rejoice; they guarantee that human beings are passionate living creatures, not entombed mummies.

His sister Maureen attempts to seal herself within the role of American wife within the sanctuary of suburbia, but Jules reminds her of her susceptibility:

".. . don't forget that this place here can burn down too. Men can come back in your life, Maureen, they can beat you up again and force your knees apart, why not? There's so much of it in the world, so much semen, so many men! Can't it happen? Won't it happen? Wouldn't you really want it to happen?"
"No!"
"Maureen, really? Tell me."
"No, never. Never" (p. 478).

Jules's insistence on an answer to his final question implies his incredulity about Maureen's self-imposed isolation. She has chosen to live in a "park," as it were, instead of within the "city" of man. But "parks won't burn!" In her attempt to escape the terror, she has also denied the joy of shared humanity. She has cut herself off both from her immediate family—even though Jules comments ironically, "But honey, aren't you one of *them* yourself?" (p. 478)—and from the larger "them," the family of man, to whom she will always be a stranger. In its insistent parallels, the novel does indeed demonstrate that "we are all members of a single human family." The common inheritance of this human family is the shared passions and emotions, the "fires" within, which Jules calls the "Spirit of the Lord."

Jules, in contrast to Maureen, regains his old self-confidence and joyfulness, his faith in his own nature, his American belief that his fortune lies ready to be made in the West, his wish to marry Nadine. He truly believes that "fire burns and does its duty," that his former life has burned away and he is ready to start anew: "Everything that happened to me before this is nothing—it doesn't exist!—my life is only beginning now" (p. 477). Although he has failed to achieve unity with Nadine, he intends to try again to make that relationship work. Although he may be opening himself to another gunshot wound, he may also be opening himself to the emotional fulfillment, the spiritual unity, he craves. Although "passion can't endure," it "will come back again and again," and he will be receptive to its cyclic return.

Clearly, Jules's answer to the question: how does one be one's self?, is to trust to the "fires" within, the inexplicable inner drives which paradoxically both make us all members of a single human family and choose—through their own complex chemistry—a unique fate for the self. Maureen extinguishes those fires in an attempt to be relieved of the burden of selfhood. But the experience of Nadine suggests that the marriage which Maureen hides behind will not shield her from the misery of an insecure and undefined self. How could she be different? How could she be like her brother? Perhaps she cannot. Perhaps her timidity and terror and her devastating experiences can never be overcome. Perhaps like her father, Howard Wendall, she is too weak to trust to and to nourish the "private, nameless kernel of the self." But perhaps her double, Nadine, will find her inner self—not because she has money or lives in a different social environment; the forces which constrict the self are primarily psychological, not sociological; inner, not outer—but because Jules sees her as his fate, and he will incessantly try to embrace that fatality. Paradoxically, freedom is found in Necessity. One is not simply free existentially to create oneself out of deliberate and conscious choices. Maureen's attempt to create a self according to a conscious plan, like Karen's, Clara's, and Nada's attempts before her, is an evasion rather than a realization of selfhood. Rather, one *must* act in accordance with one's unconscious drives through which the self expresses and defines itself. One must be true to that unique kernel of the self "which could neither be broken nor escaped from."[14] Adherence to these inner dictums is not confining, but liberating. Jules "thought of himself as a character in a book being written by himself," because his inner self is truly creating his fate. Jules is Oates's affirmative demonstration that *some* individuals, at least, are capable of full and joyful selfhood.

While the book shows how distant the lives of the poor are from the informing myths of our society and records the radical expedients they must take in order to attempt to fulfill them, yet Jules is a genuine hero, a positive character whose spirit soars despite the seemingly naturalistic determinism which would pull him down. Although he learns how to exploit the system to his own advantage, he also regains the joyful spontaneity which characterized him as a child. He emerges from his life as a punk teenager to a young man receptive to his passion for Nadine and capable of articulating his longing for spiritual union with others. Although temporarily deadened by her attempted murder and suicide, he yet is returned again through his participation in the riot to his essential self. This final novel of the trilogy, which won the 1970 National Book Award, depicts a male character finally achieving liberating selfhood through violence.

I should note that not all readers of the novel agree with this view of Jules. One critic thinks that Jules has changed from an "idealistic rebel" to "a calculating nihilist who allows himself to be recruited by the federal government for a ridiculous social program in California" and who craves Nadine out of "vengeance and quite conscious lust, having very little to do with love."[15] Many of the undergradute and graduate students at Wayne State University find him to be the same punk kid he always was, continuing to lust after the glittering life of the rich embodied in Nadine, still hopelessly naive about his ability to make his fortune in the West. That a number of readers of the novel cannot or will not recognize or value Jules's "spiritual rebirth" points to an apparent disharmony of theme and characterization at the heart of this novel—and some of the others—which I will examine more fully in the final chapter of this study.

CHAPTER 4

The Phantasmagoria of Personality: Liberation through Love

Wonderland and *Do With Me What You Will* duplicate many features characteristic of Oates's novelistic world, such as: an early scene of family violence, a male character seeking liberation from limited selfhood, a female character living passively in a fog of unrealized selfhood, the portrayal of powerful magnetism between a man and a woman offering potential liberation through love. But these latter two novels are more complex than the earlier. Within the context of successful professional lives and amid medical and legal perceptions and definitions of personality as brains diseased or healthy or as citizens guilty or not guilty, the quest for selfhood is articulated intellectually as well as experienced emotionally. Jesse of *Wonderland* is confronted with a totally phenomenological definition of human personality and Jack of *Do With Me What You Will* with a totally legalistic view of ethics and sanity. Oates begins to employ less conventional novelistic techniques than before to develop the increased complexity of her characters and the density of her subject matter. Despite some similarities between the two stories, they are radically different in tone and outcome. *Wonderland* is one of the strangest, most disturbing books in Oates's canon, depicting unrelieved suffering of identity crises on the part of nearly all the major characters, but particularly Jesse. *Do With Me What You Will*, on the other hand, is the most affirmative of her novels depicting, as no other does, achieved selfhood and liberation through love. Elena, its central female character, is the culmination and epitome of the several women without a self in Oates's novels, but she is the only one who is awakened and redeemed through love.

74

I Wonderland: *Search for a Father*

Wonderland begins with an even bigger bang than other Oatesian novels. In an early scene, Willard Harte destroys his family and himself, except for the lone survivor of the bloodbath, his son Jesse, who although wounded escapes out a back window. Jesse awakens in a hospital to begin his lifelong struggle with "the phantasmagoria of personality."[1] He changes his name to Jesse Vogel when he lives with grandfather Vogel, but he angers his grandfather by wanting to look at the stored furnishings of his family's home—the remnants of his shattered identity—and moves in for a time with his aunt and uncle, again unsuccessfully. After a short time at an orphanage, again Jesse Harte, he is taken in by the strange Dr. Pedersen, who wants to mold him into a son, indeed into his very self; and as Jesse Pedersen, the boy eagerly seeks to conform to his wishes.

Pedersen is the first in a series of successful medical men who serve as surrogate fathers and role models for Jesse. Presented in a quasi-surrealistic mode, the family dinners of the grotesquely obese Pedersens are orgies of gastronomic excess where the enormous intake of food is matched by the Pedersen children's demonstrations of prodigious intellectuality. This parody of the answer to a father's perennial dinnertime question—"What did you learn today?"— would be humorous if the father and, consequently, the children did not take the acquisition of knowledge and the development of the intellect so deadly seriously. Pedersen is an eclectic mystic-doctor-philosopher who believes in the godlike potential of the human organism. Echoing Friedrich Nietzsche's concept of the "higher man" Pedersen explains to Jesse: "To displace God is not easy. To be higher, a higher man, that is not an easy fate. And I believe you will share this fate with me" (p. 110)[2] He believes mystically that "all life is a movement into the infinite" and that man is in a friendly contest with God to usurp his place (p. 109). Man achieves his potential by ceaselessly striving to become his fullest self, the self he was fated to be. The enormous size of the Pedersens is a comic illustration of his belief that each individual human cell must strain outward. Pedersen combines his belief in Science, Fate, and God with a cosmic sense of American Manifest Destiny: "America is blessed by God. America is all men, all humanity, blessed by God and pushing outward, always outward" (p. 113). Indeed, despite his eccentricities, Pedersen is prototypically American in his disregard of the past and in his undaunted belief in progress, in self betterment, and in the unique and blessed fate of the American people. Oates is inviting us to see Pedersen as a grotesque caricature of the American spirit.

Pedersen's destructive effect upon his family becomes increasingly apparent. His philosophy sanctifies a massive egotism engulfing the other members of his family. His daughter Hilda cries, "*You want to stuff me inside your mouth. I know you! I know you!*" (p. 140). His wife desperately tries to break away from him before she loses her own separate selfhood. Jesse is to become the doctor's very self: "I have been calculating for some time, I have been planning, imagining how you will grow into my place, into my very being" (p. 98). But Jesse, unlike Hilda and Mrs. Pedersen, does not resent this usurpation of his being. He prays: "*Let me be like them, let them love me, let everybody know that I am one of them*" (p. 86). But despite his lack of rebelliousness and his servile attempt to please, his kindness and assistance to Mrs. Pedersen during her crazed, abortive escape attempt evoke the wrath of Pedersen, who severs him irrevocably from the family: "now you are eradicated by the family. Never try to contact us again. You are dead. You do not exist" (p. 184).

In Book Two Jesse, a medical student at the University of Michigan, tries to resume the identity of Jesse Vogel, but not without irreparable damage to his sense of himself: "When he began to think of himself, to contemplate himself, his entire body reacted as if in sudden panic—there were things he must not think, must not contemplate, most not remember" (p. 187). Although he suppresses the Pedersen episode, just as he has repressed his childhood trauma, he is shaped by those experiences nonetheless. He retains many of Pedersen's attitudes and even takes on some of his eccentricities: his rejection of the past, his work ethic, his faith in medicine, his obsessive need to prevent death and to run a clinic; and he finds another doctor, Cady, who uses some of the same rhetoric in his adulation of the human biological organism.

Dr. Cady's emphasis, however, is upon the machinelike perfection of the human body rather than upon the aspiring spirit. Jesse, ever malleable, is influenced by Cady's perceptions: "Yes, even his spirit was become automated, mechanized" (p. 191). Jesse now looks to Cady to supply him with a pattern for the self. But Cady also lectures upon the failure of science to explain the world outside of the perceiving senses and the relationship of the senses to the outside world (p. 194), and Jesse cannot agree that this is a viable mystery: "Isn't the great lesson of science *control?* . . . If he had control of himself, Jesse Vogel, then nothing else mattered in the universe" (p.

195). For Jesse, then, "the world" is narrowly that which one can control; all else is irrelevant and distracting. So Jesse must block troubling memories of the past and must not think about his relationship to other people, for "time was mobbed with people. How could he establish himself, construct himself in such a mob . . . ?" (p. 195). Jesse knows that he does not have complete mastery of his willed self because in parts of his brain "other Jesses existed, sinister and unkillable, and he accepted them, he could not rid himself of them" (pp. 190–91). In an attempt to latch onto normality Jesse has become engaged to a pretty nurse, Anne-Marie, but, partly through his friend Monk's apparent disapproval, he drops her and then becomes attached to Helene Cady, largely because she is Dr. Cady's daughter. Eventually marrying Helene, Jesse is more finely controlling the projected shape of his life, influenced now by Dr. Cady.

T. W. Monk, Cady's assistant, also plays a major role in Jesse's life at this stage. He is a brilliant but unstable young man who drops medicine and eventually emerges as an avant-garde poet in New York. While he has an obsessive interest in Jesse, he is in most ways his opposite. He counters Jesse's dedication to life by a wish for death (in fact, he provokes Jesse into fighting with him, knowing he has a weak heart); Jesse's compulsion for work, by his deliberate dropping out; Jesse's adulation of health, by his adulation of cancer (one of his celebrated poems is a blasphemous prayer to cancer modeled on the "Hail Mary": "the brain heaving like a penis / on unleash us! unleash us! carcinoma of / the brain hail / full of grace / now and at the hour of our birth / Amen" [p. 456]); Jesse's reverence for the human body by his desecration of it (he helps himself to a piece of human flesh in the laboratory). Monk's somewhat enigmatic function in the novel is perhaps as Jesse's alter ego, the darker self, who responds differently to the same data on human experience. Jesse chooses to ignore and, if necessary, to repress "the chaos" which Monk faces, the seething uncontrollable world outside of the narrow confines within which he is determined to guard his selfhood.

Jesse's final father-surrogate is Dr. Perrault, a celebrated brain surgeon to whom Jesse is interned and with whom he eventually practices. From Pedersen to Cady to Perrault is projected progressively a view that the concept of the human personality as fixed and knowable is illusory. Pedersen's belief in fate, that the self is ever aspiring to become the self it was fated to be and to unite with the infinite, is replaced by Cady's more modest depiction of the human organism as an extraordinarily well-functioning machine which cannot comprehend its relationship to the world outside of the senses. Perrault totally discounts the concept of personality as "just a tradition that dies hard" (p. 335). A phenomenologist who believes that the human being is merely matter—a brain, a mass of cells, which can be snuffed out in thirty seconds—he has no respect for the sanctity of the self. Perrault even believes in brain transplants, arguing that exceptional brains should be viewed as public property and not be allowed to die with the body.

Although Helene is upset over such talk which denigrates the individual and which seems to her a kind of murder, Jesse is seemingly in accord with Perrault. Without an actual transplant of Perrault's brain, Jesse takes on some of his identity: Perrault jokes that Jesse is his tall self who has part of his being memorized in his fingertips. Other internists who were not chosen to work with Perrault contemptuously remark that in doing so one becomes a copy of a copy of a human being. But Jesse seems more than a copy; he seems literally to take on Perrault's being. He feels prematurely aged by vicarious participation in Perrault's aging and uncertain of his own separate identity: "*Jesse Vogel: who was that?*" (p. 397). Medicine has intensified Jesse's personal sense of disconnection from the world, since to accept Dr. Perrault's account of human personality is to posit that the self is merely a brain with no connection to the outer world or indeed to its own body. Yeats's line, "knowledge increases unreality," an epigraph to the volume, is apt here.

Helene feels denied by Jesse's failure to "imagine" her: "She was being destroyed by her husband, she thought, annihilated by him. He could not imagine her, had not had time to imagine her existence, and so was destroying her" (p. 412). Helene is an intelligent, self-contained woman who suffers a life of quiet desperation after her marriage. She is one of many women in Oates's canon who is not comfortable with her own body. Helene does not enjoy sex and has an excessive dread of pregnancy. Miserably unhappy and sick while pregnant, she yet feels that she must undergo pregnancies for Jesse, who wants four children. Her tension and fear of sexual violation reach a grotesque extreme during a gynecological exam when she panics, thrashes her legs around, and runs out of the examination room bleeding from the internal injuries inflicted by the doctor's instrument as she struggles to release herself. Jesse respects and loves Helene, but their relationship is mutually unfulfilling. While she certainly has her own totally separate identity problems, her exclusion by Jesse intensifies her condition.

It is their daughter Shelley who feels "absorbed" by Jesse, smothered by his excessive protection and concern. Shelley feels that she exists in her father's head and he in hers: "Father you have got to let me go. You have got to stop thinking about me and let me go. You hypnotized me. I am like a deer standing in the road, hypnotized by the headlights of a car" (p. 425). In her desperation she runs away from home with a counterculture freak, Noel, who urges her to "dream back" her father, to obliterate him from memory. She writes her father long letters which, perhaps unwittingly, communicate her love and concern: *"Father, I love you I want to come back to you"* (p. 390). Nonetheless, she pursues a self-destructive course in her futile attempt to free herself from him. She drops enough clues for him to find her on Yonge Street in Toronto only after she is fatally ill with liver failure from drugs and dissipation. In the melodramatic ending of the hardback edition Jesse and Shelley are last seen aimlessly drifting in a boat, Shelley "sick, dying, he could smell the stench of death about her," and Jesse lamenting her broken and unfulfilled selfhood:

"Why are you going away from me, all of you, going away one by one . . ." he said, clutching at her, feeling her head, her dryness, her incredible dryness, the dryness of this body that was straining to get loose from him and to fly out of the world entirely: straining to break its orbit and elude him forever. Where were they all going, these people who abandoned him?—one by one, going away, abandoning him? Was there a universe of broken people, flung out of their orbits but still living was there perhaps a Jesse there already in that void, the true, pure, undefiled Jesse, who watched this struggling Jesse with pity?[3]

In the paperback edition, on the other hand, Shelley's impending death is less certain, and Jesse regains his old sense of "control": "Jesse waited for his heart to calm again. He waited for the beating to subside, for his brain to come back into control of itself: how he loved this control, this certainty!" (p. 478).[4] The two versions, then, leave us with quite a different sense of Jesse. In the original he achieves no semblance of wholeness; in the paperback he seems able to prevent his daughter's death (*"Nobody is going to die tonight. No dying tonight. Not on my hands"* [p. 478]) and to gain some measure of control over himself and the situation.

While the scene is excessively melodramatic and maudlin and unnecessarily prolonged, the first ending is preferable, for there is nothing in the second to indicate that Jesse has achieved mastery over "the phantasmagoria of personality."[5] Any "control" he exercises is as a skillful doctor, not as a wholesome individual or as a successful father. Those Oatesian characters who succeed in liberating themselves always do so by opening up to their instinctual selves, often through violence or sexual love. Jesse has a gun but he fails to use it on Noel, his daughter, or himself, although in a typically Oatesian correspondence he, like his father before him, has a moment of destructive impulse when it seems better to do away with his family than to try to live with them (p. 444). But Jesse is here as unable to commit himself to violent action as he was earlier to sexual love.

The opportunity for liberation through love comes with the "dream-girl" Reva, who first enters Jesse's life as a witness to a self-inflicted castration of a man Jesse treats at the hospital. Later, when they meet by chance on a street corner and he is powerfully attracted to her, he arranges an assignation. The meeting, however, is unsuccessful because she claims that she is involved with someone else. Sometime later she calls on him and he goes to her excitedly, only to discover that she is looking for a doctor to perform an abortion. Obsessed with Reva and feeling the potentiality of liberation through this relationship ("He felt an immense, dangerous pulsation—as if the hot, hollow, radiant core of his being, the elusive Jesse itself, were very close to his grasp" [p. 351]), Jesse journeys to northern Wisconsin, where she is staying with a group of artists. Convincing her to go away with him, he leaves for an hour to clean up and give her time to get ready. But in the motel room, he accidentally cuts himself while shaving with a rusty blade and then deliberately cuts various places of his body, including his genitals, making a return to Reva impossible. In his self-imposed bloodbath, Jesse is denying his own sexual drives, at first subconsciously then willfully. Ironically Jesse duplicates the self-maiming of the patient who first brought Reva and him together: their relationship begins and ends in slain manhood. Jesse does not achieve liberation through love; Reva remains only a dream.

The repeated references to a "platonic" Jesse suggest that Jesse, and perhaps Oates, has not completely debunked Dr. Pedersen's notion of an ideal self which the ordinary self strives to be: "Was there, in that shadow-ridden heaven, another form of Jesse too, watching him, yearning to draw up to him Jesse's hollow, radiant, yearning self? Yearning to purify himself at last, after so many years?" (p. 466). What is discredited, however. is the idea that this selfhood can be attained through intellectual striving alone. The human personality is more than mere matter, more than a mass of cells called the brain, as Dr. Perrault claims. Rather it is a mysterious fixed entity, which can be realized only when the self responds unfalteringly to its most instinctual drives, when finite man opens up to the infinite. (Indeed, the title of Book Two of the novel, which ends in Jesse's self-inflicted bloodbath, echoes Sören Kierkegaard: "The Finite Passing of an Infinite Passion.") Dr. Perrault's exaltation of the superior human brain is the extreme extension of what Oates calls elsewhere the "death throes of the Renaissance," the climate of opinion which urges man to "master everything about him, including his own private nature, his own 'ego,' redefining himself in terms of a conqueror whose territory should be as vast as his own desire to conquer."[6] Perrault, disinterested in man as a personality, a separate self, values only the all-consuming mass of cells called the brain. It is an impersonal egotism but an egotism nonetheless, an eradication of the whole personality in favor of the Faustian all-conquering intellect. It is a false ideal, an impossible goal. Man cannot achieve a sense of well-being and wholeness through intellectual "control," through deliberate and conscious choices alone. Rather, he must let go of his ego and let his "hollow, radiant, yearning self" emerge.

Jesse is desperate for connections to the world beyond the self. Like Jules Wendall of *them,* he senses a mystical unity of man, senses that "we are all members of a single human family"; and he, the child of innumerable abortive familial relationships, seeks to secure his place in that "family." But he is going about it the wrong way, trying to absorb the world and other people into himself. Rather he must lose control—lose the desire to absorb—and let the "radiant core of his being" emerge. Jesse is incapable of such an opening up to his instinctual self and thus is incapable of liberation. In the original version, finding no stability in the fluid world, he can only lament the perpetual broken communions with others. *Wonderland* is a disquieting book, as Oates herself recognizes, in which there is no resolution, no release from the straining of the central character to find himself: it is, the author observes, "the first novel I have written that doesn't end in violence, that doesn't liberate the hero through violence, and therefore there is still a sickish, despairing, confusing atmosphere about it."[7] Her later revision of the book is only confusing, however, for Jesse resumes a controlled way of coping with experience that has already proved to be unsatisfactory to both himself and his family.

II   Wonderland: *Parallels to* Alice in Wonderland

The novel is enriched through its extensive parallels to Lewis Carroll's *Alice in Wonderland and Through the Looking-Glass*, which I will only touch upon here. Oates has commented frequently upon the importance during her childhood of Carroll's tale, which she now teaches in her psychology and literature class. If Carroll's book is a "dream-vision" where Alice's "literal quest serves, vicariously, as the reader's metaphorical search for meaning in the lawless, haphazard universe of his deepest consciousness," so too is Oates's novel a dream-vision in which Jesse is plunged into the abyss of "the phantasmagoria of personality." Both characters have a symbolic birth into a world of chaos which defies a "logical, orderly, and coherent approach to the world."[8] Alice's fall down the rabbit hole, her suspension in a pool of tears, and her small size when passing through the door of Wonderland can be viewed as symbolic insemination, gestation in amniotic fluid, and finally birth.[9] Oates uses some of the same images[10] as Jesse bursts through the window of his blood-soaked home, attempting to elude his gun-toting father:

Jesse steps forward suddenly into the blood. Through the blood. His feet carry him through it and something is knocked over—a splintering crash—and Jesse is at the bedroom door now and fumbling with the doorknob, getting it open. Jesse . . . throws himself against the window. Everything bursts—it gives way—comes apart as if in a dream. Jesse falls through the window, covering his face with his hands, and then he is outside and running (p. 43).

Stripped of their previous identities, Alice and Jesse are, in effect, like infants; only now—deprived of maternal nurturance—they are all alone in worlds of frightening metamorphosis and incipient extinction of being, worlds governed by quixotic principles and authorities. Mad, morphine-hooked Dr. Pedersen finds his counterparts in the Mad Hatter and the hookah-smoking Caterpillar of Carroll's Wonderland, both who imperiously demand that Alice "explain" herself as Pedersen does Jesse. Pedersen's monstrous egg-like appearance and know-it-all attitude also recall Humpty-Dumpty. Mrs. Pedersen, in turn, is the passionate Red Queen who brings "chaos" into the Pedersen household (according to her daughter Hilda) and who drags Jesse back and forth to Buffalo, as the Red Queen drags Alice through the air, in her frenzied attempt to escape from her husband and to secure her lover-like son. As Alice may at any moment unwittingly evoke the Queen of Hearts' wrathful "off with her head," so too must Jesse face repeatedly the threat of extinction effected through the murderous despair of his father Willard Harte, the annihilating dismissal of Dr. Pedersen, the contemptuous indifference of Dr. Perrault.

As an infant in the oral phase of libidinal development[11] imperfectly distinguishes between itself and the world and attempts to take in the whole world through its mouth, so too is oral incorporation a vehicle of identity in these worlds, only here it has a disturbingly metamorphic effect. As Alice changes in size through eating from very large to very small, so too does Jesse swell while under the tutelage of the grossly obese Pedersens, and then shrink again when he is dismissed by Dr. Pedersen as "dead." In both instances changes in size represent changes in identity, shattering any sense of permanent identity. Indeed, Alice's tortuous question: "But if I'm not the same, the next question is "Who in the world am I? Ah, *that's* the great puzzle!," is echoed again and again by Jesse: "Sometimes he felt a flurry of panic to think that he was nothing at all, that he did not exist. What did that mean—*to exist?* . . . He did not understand. It made no sense" (p. 73).

A number of psychoanalysts have noted the preponderance of "oral trauma" or "oral sadistic trends of a cannibalistic nature"[12] in Carroll's work; indeed, this is the quality which Oates herself underscores in her reading of Carroll,[13] and it is in this respect that her work most strikingly parallels the *Alice* books. For in both Wonderlands not only are fantastic rituals of eating given prominent focus—the Mad Tea-Party and the family dinners of the Pedersens—but cannibalization is a literal or figurative possibility: these are worlds of frightening, ubiquitous oral aggression where people and creatures "eat each other up" in the often absurd yet deadly serious game of survival. As the child in the later oral phase thinks of mouths as a threat imagining himself devouring or being devoured, so too is nearly every page of Carroll's Wonderland infused with creatures eating or being eaten, and Oates's novel with "images of the mouth—and with related images of wombs, sacs, boxes, shells, and cells."[14] As the Walrus and the Carpenter devour their dinner guests, the Oysters, Hilda claims her father wants "*to eat us all up!*" (p. 140); Pedersen sanguinely plots his usurpation of Jesse's separate selfhood; Monk helps himself to a piece of human flesh from the laboratory where medical research routinely desecrates cadavers of human beings and carcasses of animals; Perrault advocates "brain transplants"; and Jesse "introjects" bits of his "fathers," daughter, patients, medical knowledge into his brain tissue in a desperate attempt to keep the world and people from "going away" from him, much like the infant who is developing a generalized mistrust of his source of nurturance clamps down on the quixotic breast to secure it to himself. Jesse's massive introjection causes his wife Helene to question whether a person can be biologically as well as psychologically multiple: " 'I don't mean people who think they are more than one person, but people who really are multiple. Real units of personality, tissue or atoms or nerve cells,' she said vaguely, wildly, 'bits of flesh that are real and not imaginary, not insane' " (p. 422). Indeed, Jesse asserts that Dr. Perrault "exists in me, in my brain. In certain cells in my brain" (p. 411). "Pieces" of Dr. Pedersen's philosophy show up as unassimilated lumps of Jesse's character later in his life. His daughter Shelley becomes "not the girl Shelley, but rather the ghostly 'scan' of his own brain . . . a posterior frontal tumor in Dr. Vogel's brain" (pp. 441-42), paralleling Tweedledum and Tweedledee's insistence that Alice is just a part of the Red King's dream. As Alice thinks that the Red King might be, after all, a part of *her* dream, so too is Jesse a part of Shelley's who feels she must "dream back" the nightmare of Jesse walking around in her head; for in his frenzied desire to save Shelley, Jesse has created a nightmarish Wonderland for her where he is likened to the Red Queen pulling her through the air (p. 401).

Perhaps the most persistent similarity of Jesse and Alice is their ineffectual attempts to control the phantasmagoria in which they find themselves by imposing order upon it. Likewise, each work has a character who thoroughly embraces the chaotic and irrational: the smiling, vanishing Cheshire Cat who declares "we're all mad here" finds his parallel in genial, enigmatic T. W. Monk who celebrates the chaos and the cancer that Jesse would control.[15] As Alice struggles against the destructive world of Wonderland with her concepts of propriety and logic, Jesse tries with medical expertise and introjection of others into his brain tissue to prevent disorder, separation, and death. Ironically, while each becomes a success in the Chessboard worlds they enter—Alice becomes a Queen, Jesse a famous neurosurgeon—they bring into these worlds more chaos and disorder than they dispel. Alice, for example, floods Wonderland with her tears, disrupts the jurymen with her monstrous size, provokes a pack of cards to revolt against her, destroys the Looking-Glass world with a yank of the tablecloth. Jesse, too, "ruined things, made people jumpy and awkward" (p. 68): he provokes Monk to fight with him; exacerbates his wife's suppressed hysteria and feeling of disconnection by his withdrawal from her; drives his daughter to her frenetic flight from sanity, order, connection, and control by his claustrophobic "love." Finally, though, just as Alice flees from "the frightening anarchy of the world underneath the ground of common consciousness"[16] and wakes up, Jesse rejects the alternate dream-vision of Reva, who represents the chaotic, uncontrolled world of the unconscious, and who might have opened him up to the "elusive Jesse" within. In the hardback edition, at the end of the novel Jesse is caught in the dream, puzzled by his persistent failure to control experience and other people, whereas in the revised paperback version he achieves—rather unconvincingly—the superficial victory of Alice. As Alice dismisses the "insoluble problem of meaning in a meaningless world"[17] with her waking-world resumption of insight, logic, and control: "You're nothing but a pack of cards!", so too Jesse "awakens," dismissing Noel, Shelley's lover, and resuming control of his daughter and himself. Just as the reader is impressed by the figurative reality of Alice's dream-vision, so too is he struck by Oates's nightmarish depiction of Jesse's disorientation. The difference is that in Oates's work, unlike Carroll's, the dream is not one from which one can so facilely awaken.

Although the book is focused primarily upon individuals—particularly Jesse—it suggests a breadth of reference beyond individual lives—"Wonder-World" in W. H. Auden's phrase.[18] "Wonderland" in "T. W. Monk's" poem[19] which prefaces the volume is the human eye with which the self strives to orient itself; and "Wonderland East" is the shopping center—emblem of an ugly, materialistic society with its "concrete square—cheaply decorated with 'modern' multicolored cubes and benches of garish carnival colors" (p. 417) where Helene meets her would-be lover. More broadly "Wonderland" is American society where a poor boy whose father destroyed his family can become a famous surgeon, but where the individual personality cannot keep up with the radical displacements that such a Horatio Algeresque rise entails. Oates handles personality better than sociology, so that the strain is discernible when she attempts generalization.

Weakest is the third and final book of the novel, "Dreaming America," which abruptly thrusts us into the world of the counterculture and suggests that President Kennedy's assassination in 1963 signaled the break-up of settled, ordered, directed society and initiated the malaise which afflicted the youth of the Sixties. Shelley is

abnormally upset over the president's death, a concern less credible
than her fixation on her overly protective father. The young take to
the streets, display an impersonal hatred of the older generation, and
display a disturbing uniformity so that hundreds of girls in Chicago
could be Jesse's daughter and all the young people seem to exist "as if
in a dream, having no center to them, no core, no place to get to" (p.
465). Oates is suggesting that the society suffers from the same violent
loss of a "father" in President Kennedy that Jesse did in the loss of his
parent and, consequently, suffers compositely from the same disorientation; but the parallel is somewhat forced. In truth, Jesse's
experiences are unique, not universal. Comparatively few individuals must endure the murderous destruction of their immediate
families, and very few have experiences at all comparable to those of
Jesse with the Pedersens. It is not the typical American who becomes
a famous brain surgeon and who complicates his life by probing the
brain both surgically and intellectually.

But although the novel is weaker in its final section and less
convincing in its breadth of reference than in its portrayal of
individual characters, yet one can appreciate the ambition and artistic
neatness of Oates's attempted correspondences, where man's attempt to live in his body parallels his attempt to live in society; where
cancerous growths are biological and sociological; where personal
problems reflect social movements; personal tragedy, national
tragedy; the death of a father, the death of a president. Always fond
of realistic details like references to public personalities, historical
events, and specific localities, Oates is more successful in this
particular novel when she moves into the realm of the semihallucino-
genic. The Pedersen episode is masterfully expressionistic rather
than realistic. The contest of mathematical wizardry in which Hilda
devours a mound of candy bars to feed her remarkable brain is a
superb blend of the bizarre and the pathetic. Here Oates breaks the
third-person narration for the immediacy of Hilda's response which
includes poignantly her schizophrenic withdrawal from her father's
constant pressure: "*Hilda lays her head on Father's shoulder and
sleeps. I do not sleep. I do not think. I am dead*" (p. 142). In her next
novel, *Do With Me What You Will*, Oates becomes increasingly
experimental in the use of point of view and time sequences, significantly heightening the effectiveness of her narration. *Wonderland* is
not the most pleasing of Oates's novels in its subject and in its form,
but it stands at the center of her work as the most unrelenting

depiction of an individual unable to cope with the phantasmagoria of personality.

III   Do With Me What You Will: *Law versus Love*

In *Do With Me What You Will*, the most affirmative novel to date in Oates's canon, law rather than medicine provides the constructs with which and against which the individual seeks definition. But just as medicine fails to provide a satisfactory explanation and definition of the individual personality and its relationship to others in *Wonderland*, so too in this novel the law cannot truly determine guilt or innocence, sanity or insanity, justice or injustice, dealing as it does not with living personalities but with "fictions," constructs of those personalities fashioned by lawyers bent on conviction or acquittal. Despite the omnipresence of law, the selfhood finally achieved by the two main characters, Jack and Elena, is totally divorced from a legalistic framework. Love, not law, becomes the vehicle of liberation.

The lives of Elena and Jack are initially presented separately; Part One focuses on Elena's experiences, and Part Two, on Jack's. The structure of the novel, however, serves to parallel and counterpoint these episodes and to highlight the importance of the pair's first meeting. Each section begins with a traumatic childhood experience involving criminal action by a father: Elena's father kidnaps her from school, and Jack's father kills a man. Each section traces subsequent important events including marriages—Elena marrying Marvin Howe, the lawyer who defended Jack's father. Finally each section ends with the first meeting of the two characters when Elena stands immobilized in front of a statue in downtown Detroit and Jack attempts to awaken her from her stupor.

For each character the childhood trauma has a formative effect. Elena, who had obediently remained still in the dark for hours to evade detection when with her crazed father, retains, after she is returned to her mother, an exaggerated passivity and fearful withdrawal from experience. She regains her speech with difficulty, fears the dark, exercises caution in even the most mundane details of living, and morbidly identifies with victims of accidental deaths. Even when seemingly "normal," she remains excessively moldable and obedient to her shrewd and opportunistic mother, Ardis. When Ardis tells Elena that she is as peaceful as a statue, divorced from the aggression of ordinary people, Elena acquiesces readily to the description of this soporific state: *"I looked down upon my own body and saw that it had gone into stone"* (p. 106).[20]

Elena's husband, Marvin Howe, as he later explains to her, is attracted to her otherworldly quality, her being seemingly so untouched by the corruption of the world: "you're someone in a vacuum, you're from the outside of everything that's physical and degrading" (p. 532). The problem, of course, with being so peacefully outside of the world is that Elena has no connection to it. She has a hand in the usual activities of a suburban matron: she entertains, attends charitable functions, takes classes, even receives letters from her husband's mistress, but nothing creates in Elena any stirring of "life." Indeed, as Part One ends, she is stuck in time and place, a self without a selfhood, imitating the perfection and permanence of the statue before her:

A skin marked by tears, turning slowly greenish-gray. Gone into perfect hardness. Yes. She feels very well now, very happy. Yes, yes, everything has come to rest, in perfection it comes to rest, permanent.
1:45.
Stopped.
Permanent.
1:45.
Stuck. She does not move. (pp. 164–65)

In contrast, Jack's trauma as a child catapults him into action rather than passivity. He becomes fascinated with the law through his dealings with Marvin Howe, his father's defense attorney. This vital and brilliant man whom Jack simultaneously loves and hates becomes a role model and surrogate father. Later in the novel Jack spouts some of the same rhetoric about the law that Howe had earlier articulated. Both men feel that "the Law is permanent and will save us" (p. 403). Both revere, respect, and refuse to violate the structure of the law, although both care little about the absolute guilt or innocence of their clients.

But perhaps because Jack's real father, Joseph Morrissey, committed murder out of a sense of social inequity—he felt that his victim, Ned Stehlin, was responsible for his son's death and further that he had snubbed him an an inferior—Jack, unlike Howe, becomes involved in civil-rights action. Jack begins his legal practice in the South, attempting to work for equal justice for blacks. Later in

Detroit he gains a reputation for being the lawyer of the misfits and underprivileged. Jack's wife Rachel, a dedicated civil-rights worker, questions, however, the sincerity of Jack's commitment to the issues of social justice which so fires her group of friends. She senses, as he does himself, that his true joy is in the exercise of his own power to manipulate the law toward prescribed ends.

Rachel, who believes that man should act in accordance with a higher law of ethics, does not share Jack's respect for the law: "the law is dead. It's dead. It's dessicated, rotten, dead" (p. 287). Indeed, in any absolute sense justice is not achieved through law in the novel. Jack and his associates are unable to advance the cause of equity for blacks in the South; Jack's father, acquitted of murder on the grounds of temporary insanity, is very likely guilty of premeditated murder; Jack's favorite clients are those who are guilty because they are more readily pliant to the needs of his defense; a father who murdered his daughter and her friends because he disapproved of their life-style is sentimentally acquitted in Detroit (pp. 420–21);[21] and finally, in the case which upsets Jack's faith in his skill and luck as a lawyer, Mered Dawe, an eccentric antimaterialist who preaches transcendent love, is convicted on a trumped-up charge of possession of marijuana.[22] The "salvation" inherent in the law, so touted by both Howe and Jack, is ephemeral. But love, an unrealized dream in *Wonderland*, becomes a reality in this novel. Jack and especially Elena are "saved" through the liberating power of love.

Mered Dawe, a kind of modern-day Christ, who is "crucified" by the law for his rantings about love, serves to unite the two dominant concerns of the novel, law and love. Although it is perhaps unwise to give too much weight to his preachings, Mered has a significant effect on Elena, who attends one of his lectures and visits him with Jack in the hospital after he is beaten in the violent break-up of the meeting. Believing in the power of love to absorb and transform hate, Mered proclaims the supremacy of "mind-stuff" over matter. While in the hospital, Mered, feeling powerfully drawn to Elena and Jack, wants the three of them to be united in love. He says to Elena: " 'You could love both of us; you could love everyone. . . . No, don't let her go,' he said when Jack released her. 'Why did you do that? That was so nice, that was lovely, I really could feel you touching her and I could feel myself touched by you' " (p. 438). Although Jack jokingly breaks this chain of feeling, Elena is moved by the experience. Later, after Mered's case is "solved" and he is put away in prison, she thinks about the power of his love: "She thought of Mered's embrace, the calm intimacy of his arms, his face, his presence. He might have united them all—himself and Jack united in her" (p. 513).

Mered is instrumental in helping to awaken Elena from her state of passive nonfeeling, but much more significant is her love of Jack. Whereas Sleeping Beauty was awakened by the prince with a kiss, this modern-day sleeper is not so easily aroused. Only when she chances to experience orgasm, long after her affair with Jack has begun, does Elena awaken to emotional life.

Part Three of the novel, entitled "Crime" (in this ironic novel, love is repeatedly a crime), traces the adulterous relationship of Jack and Elena from their unusual meeting in front of the statue in downtown Detroit through the vicissitudes of their affair. While both are aware of a powerful attraction at this first meeting, Elena resists his initial overture. One day while in California, however, acting on impulse, she phones him and he flies from Detroit to be with her. Although he responds to her passionately, she remains in a vacuous state. Nonetheless, though she doubts her selfhood, Elena believes in their attraction: "She loved him. What had happened was real, even if she herself were not real" (p. 336). After she experiences orgasm, however, a permanent change comes over her. Home in her bedroom she "thought with sudden elation: *This is the last time I will sleep here*" (p. 373). Although not literally true, she will not return to that deathly sleep of Sleeping Beauty. She feels the stirring of new life within her, the equivalent of a "pregnancy" which she cannot control or deny (p. 376).

But Elena does try to deny this feeling and to return to her selfless void, nearly driving Jack into a murderous rage. At the end of Part Three she returns ill and suicidal to her husband. In Part Four Marvin takes Elena to Maine in an attempt to nurse her back to health and to obliterate Jack from her memory; but Elena realizes with growing clarity that she cannot return to her former stupor: "She was awake. She realized that everything is awake, the universe is awake; that it cannot be escaped" (p. 511). While she loves and respects her husband, she is physically repulsed by him and no longer able simply to withdraw. She must leave him to affirm her own life. She takes on a hardness and a self-determination that she was incapable of before. She becomes the aggressor in the love relationship with Jack. She goes to his apartment and waits for him outside. At the end of the novel, with a look "of pure kinship, of triumph" (p. 541), they embark on their new life together.

This uncharacteristically happy ending is the first successful liberation through love in Oates's novelistic world. Perhaps the book is dedicated to Patricia Hill Burnett, a former beauty queen turned feminist, because Oates wants us to view Elena's awakening as an emblem for all women's liberation. While the orgasmic awakening of Sleeping Beauty has its witty dimension, it may evoke no humor in a dedicated feminist who believes that women can find selfhood without male assistance. But Oates views the libidinal drive as dominant for all human beings—women and men—no matter how they may seek to suppress it. Fulfillment in Oates's works, as in D. H. Lawrence's, can only come when a man and a woman can open themselves up to the emotional and biological drives within themselves; ironically only when they risk loss of control, loss of conscious self, do they have a chance of liberating the true self within. Such a risk is frightening, and many people are incapable of it. Women in particular—biologically receptive rather than aggressive, schooled in passivity—frequently perfect a state of withdrawal, nonfeeling, in which they do not risk the frightening loss of control but in which they perpetuate a selfless void. This death-in-life is the condition of Maureen *(them)* and Karen *(With Shuddering Fall)*; Nadine *(them)*, Helene *(Wonderland)*, and Shelley *(Wonderland)* are more aware and uncomfortable with their vacuousness. Elena, Oates's most extreme portrayal of immobility and nonfeeling, is awakened initially through her relationship with Jack, but subsequently through her own determined effort to find herself and to live aggressively. Oates takes care to show that Elena's growing consciousness does not depend upon Jack for its completion. Elena views her new aggression as usurping the traditional male prerogative and it offends her feminine sensibilities somewhat, yet she delights in the experimental nature of her impending activities. No longer seeking to freeze into permanence, she welcomes the unpredictability of life, "the possibility of getting him, even the possibility of not getting him" (p. 525). This receptivity to life's risks, this relishing of freedom, is a sign of her genuine liberation. With Elena, Oates is showing that women can break out of stultifying sexual stereotypes and approach life with zestful independence.

Elena's experimental approach to life is complemented by Oates's experimental novelistic techniques. Most successful is the effect of the variation of point of view and time perspective upon the perception of events. Oates's characteristic third-person narration tends toward monotony in long stretches. In this novel much more frequently than in earlier ones she intersperses snatches of first-person monologue or dialogue. Most commonly these are bits of apparent conversations of Elena and Jack at undefined times subsequent to the final scene of the novel. This technique has the advantage of providing a dual perspective upon the events—the immediacy of the third-person narration supplemented by the intimacy of the first-person recollection. This is particularly effective, for example, with Elena's experience hiding out with her father, where the trauma is portrayed from the outside and the inside, as reported and as experienced. But even more importantly, the technique reinforces the theme by providing a fuller appreciation of the success of Elena and Jack's union: people overcome the isolation of self not only by sharing their experiences in the present, but also by reliving their lives together through retelling. The dialogue interspersed throughout the book foreshadows the happy ending.

Another instance of technique complementing meaning is the final chapter of Part One, entitled "Sixteen Unrelated Time-Durations," in which brief, disconnected scenes from Elena's married life effectively show her growing disconnectedness from reality while she is engaged in seemingly normal activities. The final scene of the chapter occurs when time literally freezes for Elena at 1:45 P.M., Monday, April 12, 1971. That Oates simultaneously freezes the action at this point and then presents Jack's life up until this moment in Part Two is a particularly appropriate use of her characteristic method of suspending the action at climactic points. She uses the technique again later when Elena calls on Jack, continuing to parallel the lives of these two main characters and to highlight converging moments.

Augmenting the focus on the law is the legalistic structure of the novel where the parts are given titles reminiscent of a courtroom presentation:

PART ONE   *Twenty-eight Years, Two Months, Twenty-six days*

PART TWO   *Miscellaneous Facts, Events, Fantasies, Evidence Admissible and Inadmissible*

PART THREE   *Crime*

THE SUMMING UP

The effect of this imposition of a legalistic format is ironic, pointing up structurally as well as thematically the inadequacy of the law to define or describe experience. The law fails to measure justice or injustice, guilt or innocence, sanity or insanity, right or wrong; the characters share in a common criminality from kidnapping to murder, embezzling to adultery, entrapment to misrepresentation of facts; ironically the central "crime" of the novel, adultery, is life-affirming. The title—"do with me what you will"—a passive inversion of the legal plea *nolo contendere* (1 do not wish to contend), appropriately describes the sleeping Elena. She rejects the plea upon awakening to her full "criminality."

Do With Me What You Will, then, is more satisfying in its resolution than *Wonderland*. A weakness of the novel, however, is that its fairy-tale dimension jars with its realistic setting. Elena's Sleeping-Beauty vacuousness is not totally credible, nor are some of the details in the working out of her romance with Jack, particularly his flight to California to be with her after a slight acquaintance. Furthermore, some of my friends and students have argued that Elena's awakening to selfhood through orgasm can only be a mockery, because there is so little evidence—outside of her final pursuit of Jack—of her doing *anything* independent of other people. While I agree that Elena's credibility as a character is open to question—she is not sufficiently particularized as an "awakened" individual—the central movement of the novel, it seems to me, is not. The novel is an explicit demonstration of the liberating power of love, an implicit possibility in a number of Oates's other works. Somewhat sentimentalized, the novel contradicts those who would label Oates a congenitally morbid and pessimistic writer. This affirmation, however, does not persist in her next novel, *The Assassins*.

CHAPTER 5

The Fragmented Self: The Quest for Oneness

ALTHOUGH *The Assassins* and *Childwold* continue Joyce Carol Oates's relentless preoccupation with the nature of selfhood, these ambitious, experimental novels in many ways radically depart from her preceding ones, and they most clearly dramatize the dominant theme of her recent critical writing: "the human ego has too long imagined itself the supreme form of consciousness in the universe."[1] In both books there are intimations of a larger Self which encompasses the ego personality, indeed all of life, in a mystical oneness. The characters are both separate personalities and fragments of a disunified whole; they function both as "real" people and as psychological projections of and archetypes for one another. In both books Oates abandons entirely the third-person, omniscient narration characteristic of much of her novelistic craft for techniques grounding the narration within the consciousness of her characters. While the books have a number of similarities thematically and technically, they diverge in spirit. *The Assassins* is a grim book offering no hope for the tormented incompleteness of its characters, while *Childwold* is infused with a sense of the continuities of life; its characters have momentary experiences of transcendence of the isolated self.

I The Assassins: *Psychological Drama*

The central character of *The Assassins* is dead when the novel begins. Andrew Petrie, an ex-senator, writer, lecturer, and public figure, is the apparent victim of an assassin's bullet; the novel traces the repercussions of his death upon his wife and two brothers. *The Assassins* is in some ways reminiscent of William Faulkner's *The Sound and the Fury*, projecting the "story" as it does through the conflicting and disordered recollections, reactions, and rationalizations of three disturbed family members—first Hugh, then Yvonne, and finally Stephen—preoccupied with their interrelationships, with an absent fourth family member (Andrew), and with the dead past. It also ends with a survivor (Stephen) who is capable of only aimless existence.

Technically intricate and thematically complex, this novel is unfortunately not as illuminating as a reader would wish, even after repeated readings, because at critical junctures one is not given enough guidance through a Jungian maze. Critical facts remain obscure; dreams merge indistinguishably with reality; dreams are open to a wide range of interpretation; and the characters bear weighty symbolic burdens which sometimes defy both understanding and credibility. Most reviewers failed to realize that Andrew disguised his suicidal death as an assassination, a fact which obviously makes an enormous difference in the way one perceives and evaluates character and action. Since this fact is clearly hinted at in Andrew's final conversation with his brother Stephen near the end of the novel, the writer cannot fairly be blamed for her readers' inattention. Yet the novel is too easily misread or incompletely understood. Another fact that has also eluded reviewers is that Yvonne's "murder" and "dismemberment" do not really happen.[2] Although the text seems to indicate that she awakens from her dream, goes outside, and encounters two "murderers," apparently her dream continues to the end of Part Two. What happens is thus presented in the form of a psychological, not literal, drama—as is indeed true of much of the novel.

Andrew Petrie is not likely to warm the liberal imagination. Although allegedly attractive, charismatic, and intelligent, he is an ultraconservative whose social and political theories would deny the sanctity and rights of the individual in favor of the preservation of tradition, custom, and law and order. The individual always must be seen "in its larger category, always dwarfed and quieted by history, by the universal. Subjectivity was repellent to him" (p. 303).[3] He counters the sentimentality of liberals with hard-line authoritarianism. In fact "control" is the key to his personal as well as political philosophy. He would deny the emotional life: *"the rational side of mankind* [was] *the only sacred side . . . the future of mankind was only through reason, logic, awakened capacities in the brain that were now dormant in nearly everyone"* (p. 316). His relationship with his wife, Yvonne, is based on intellectual rapport, rather than emotional and sexual union. He turns from politics to philosophy because he believes that the "truth" must be given "perfect form." He dreams of writing a philosophical treatise which "would change our lives."

But Andrew has difficulty sustaining his impassioned quest for the truth. Subject to severe spells of depression, he periodically must refrain like an invalid from all activity. Tempted by beauty, by the natural world outside of his ego-control, he tries to close off rather than to respond to these promptings from his unrealized self. His conflict is dramatized in an experience he recollects for Yvonne. Taking a break from his writing, he had walked out along the river bank and studied a tree: *"I was amazed at its size and complexity . . . eight main trunks and they divide into twelve or thirteen smaller trunks, each large and sturdy enough to be, to have been, separate trees. It was colossal . . . astonishing . . . mysterious. One tree, or many? Many trees competing for moisture, or a single tree, nourished by a single source? It was beautiful, a monster. Fascinating"* (p. 373). The tree, a symbol for the unified self,[4] is here rather obviously a visual replica of the oneness underlying the apparent multiplicity of life, yet Andrew cannot simply accept the single unity of the tree, and he is annoyed that he *"wasted an hour or more standing at it, contemplating it. . . . Yvonne, beauty is preposterous; it has no point. It exults in itself, wasting our time, wasting our lives!"* (p. 373). He seeks to live in the world of time and consciousness, in effect, to live as one of "many trees competing for moisture" rather than to identify with the single tree. It is not surprising that the truth he wishes to express keeps "breaking into bits." Indeed, some of his notes which Yvonne sorts through after his death are characterized by repeated, totally contradictory epigrams. For example, "Individual rights are not to be thwarted by the State. . . . People are a great beast and must be governed. . . . An organization of the world's true leaders should be created. . . . Abortion is always and forever immoral and illegal. . . . World government is world tyranny. . . . The beast must not be allowed to continue to breed" (p. 403). This long list of blatant contradictions is a sign of his growing inability to accomplish the task he has set for himself.

Stephen, through his clairvoyant capacities, hears his brother's unarticulated plea for help and ineffectually comes to his aid. Psychically he "tunes-in" a dream which has puzzled Andrew. In this dream Andrew envisioned a city half-submerged by the sea, possessing no sign of life. As he wades along the street, he comes across a small animal which turns into an infant. He has a desperate desire to save the infant from drowning (pp. 391–92). Stephen realizes that Andrew's "infant" is, upon closer examination, actually some papers. The "infant," an archetypal image of man's "original, unconscious, and instinctive state . . . whose purpose is to compensate or correct, in a meaningful manner, the inevitable one-sidedness and extravagance of the conscious mind,"[5] is reduced, in other words, to "papers," Andrew's philosophical treatise. Andrew mistakenly values his work more than his infantile, unrealized self. Indeed, he confesses to Stephen that when he had once before sunk into despair, his hope was to preserve his work from disparagement by his intended suicide. He made *"fantastic plans, of acting without being discovered . . . of acting in such a way, so cunning a way, that I would never be discovered and my immense contribution to American political and philosophical thought would not be discredited"* (p. 553). But before this planned death transpires, he recovers and continues on as before. But he suggests that if the despair returns, he would reinstate his plans, a disclosure which strongly implies that he was not a victim of assassination, but of suicide: *"Self-murder. Murder of one's self. One must die and there is no one to commit the act—no one. No one else"* (p. 555). Andrew was apparently so committed to his ideas that he was willing to sacrifice his own life to preserve them. His wife, Yvonne, carries his despair a step further by seeing the ultimate meaninglessness of words and the emptiness of Andrew's prized rationality.

While her husband lives, Yvonne shares his ideas and concerns; and when he dies she attempts at first to continue his work. Like Andrew she finds "the personal life is over" (p. 262), and like him she places a high value on intellectual "control" of both personal and public life. She deliberately puts a distance between herself and other people: "she could usually retreat, observe, perform as she thought it best to perform, all the while intensely awake, passing judgment. She was in control then, always in control" (p. 298). She is opposed to love because "that hallucinatory chaos . . . was dangerous, ungovernable" (p. 298). She fears any expression of spontaneity. For example, a young black boy beating a drum with uninhibited delight so disturbs her that she faints. She has an excessive fear of becoming vulnerable to danger by not constantly guarding against potential enemies. She compiles for the authorities after Andrew's death a list of his enemies which is ludicrously inclusive—everyone is The Enemy.

In identifying herself so totally with her dead husband and his
self-destructive pursuits, she too takes on an aura of deathliness which
both surviving brothers sense at the funeral and which inspires in
each an ineffectual desire to save her. But in her icy hysteria, she is
incapable of emotional feeling or reciprocal compassion. Im-
mediately after Andrew's death she pokes her hand with a pair of
scissors in an attempt to overcome her debilitating paralysis. Chroni-
cally frigid, she drifts into sexual liaisons apparently out of an
impersonal contempt for men and as a kind of revenge against
Andrew's enemies,[6] especially his cousin Harvey, whose laborious
and unsuccessful attempt at sexual completeness is met with her
patient indifference. Indeed, one implication of the ring of snakes she
wears is that she delights in the control of men; sexually she has them
literally around her finger.[7]

Her increasing disconnectedness from life is apparent in her
relationships with other people and in her dream images. Pamela,
Andrew's second cousin who bravely and pathetically puts on a
cosmetic face and follows a starvation diet to hide her telltale aging,
functions as a shadow self of Yvonne. Although Pamela's brassy and
theatrical, extroverted manner contrasts sharply with Yvonne's elegant, introverted composure, both protect themselves with masks,
and both, in idealizing and identifying with the dead Andrew,
augment their dispossession from the living world. Pamela tells
Yvonne, "Both of us are so cold! . . . our fingernails are turning blue,
just look! We're so cold, so icy . . . *he* has us, don't you think? . . . *he*
has us" (p. 363). But Yvonne can neither reciprocally confirm the
bond that Pamela feels nor recognize her own dangerously self-
destructive idolatry of Andrew that Pamela intimates. She projects
everything negative onto other people, the environment, The
Enemy, "the other," rather than seeing it as emanating from within
herself.[8]

Yvonne's life reaches a crisis when Hugh unwittingly overdoses her
with drugs by doping her drink, and she is subjected to psychotic
hallucinations. One recurrring nightmare involves the break-up of
the carpet into corpses which are seething with maggots. She
attempts to scream for her husband "but it was a word, it could not
force itself into being" (p. 380). She cannot impose a human order—a
word—upon the impersonal cycle of nature—the maggots, the grass,
and the river. She feels nothing but alienation from life's natural
processes. She hates Andrew's farm and especially its garden of
unruly vegetation. She angrily attempts to hoe it into shape.

Furthermore, she is obsessed with a recurrent dream in which Andrew, hoeing in the garden, calls to her to come out to him, looking blind and shrunk with an artificially colored face "of liverish pink, putty and paint and darkened eyebrows" (p. 341). Although his face is so fearfully unnatural, she goes to him without hesitation, signaling her willingness to follow him into death.

Gradually she loses her desire to carry on with Andrew's work, realizing more and more the emptiness of words, the meaningless-ness of existence, the sameness of everyone: "his death does not matter, his murderers do not matter, his enemies are everywhere but none of them matter . . . they do what they must do, they say the things they must say, but they mean nothing by it . . . they are no different from him . . . they are the same person . . . the same words . . . we are all the same person, the same words" (p. 428). After this devastating epiphany, she wanted only for "everything to end."

Having lost faith in the hectic, "useful" life she has been attempting to sustain since Andrew's death, she leaves her apartment, sends off the key, and goes to Andrew's farm. Her final archetypal dream dramatizes her own deliberate self-destructiveness, her choice of death over life, Andrew over Stephen, alienation rather than integra-tion with the world beyond the self-conscious ego. She, like Andrew, is broken rather than restored by the confrontation with the inadequa-cy of her ego-bound world. She too fails to achieve individuation,[9] fails to reconcile the unconscious with the conscious self. She is at first overcome with her feeling of total isolation. Andrew has dropped away from her, the shadow of death is expelled like an aborted fetus (pp. 434–35). But she overestimates her separation from her hus-band's deathliness.

She sees a rabbit, symbol of life and fertility, in the wild garden, but her mind—unresponsive to these natural elements—returns obsessively to the dream where Andrew calls her out to himself. She also recalls her recurrent vision of a figure who appears to be Stephen, standing by a stranger's grave "holding in one hand gardening shears and in the other a spray of tiny white blossoms" (p. 435), but she turns from this ambiguous figure who holds life in balance, this Christlike figure who symbolizes the Self,[10] and runs to Andrew, who prefigures death with his horribly artificial face. Stephen has elsewhere been associated with a spray of blossoms, with the bloom of health, with the potentially restorative powers of Christ. But Yvonne rejects all this for her bond to the dead Andrew. Later a nightbird, symbol of the world of spirit, fails to hold her attention:

"That world had veered away from her now and she felt nothing for it, no passion, no anger, not even curiosity" (p. 436). Apparently still dreaming, she imagines leaving the house and encountering two men, one who still reminds her of Stephen. She is troubled by something she would like to figure out—she is, it seems, vaguely aware of the salvation implicit in the Stephen figure, but unable to respond to it. Rather she rejects any identification with the cyclical return of spring: "As Andrew had said so wisely, it was irrelevant; all of nature was irrelevant; its beauty and power were therefore arrogant, horrible" (p. 438). At the end of the dream she envisions her own brutal death and dismemberment, clinging in her dream to her conception of "they" as The Enemy antagonistic to the self, whereas in truth her assassin, like Andrew's, is within.

The pervasive self-destructiveness of the Petries is also played out in the life of Hugh, the brother whose first-person narrative, initiating the novel, contributes in large measure to the book's tedium. He is a tiresome, whiny, garrulous person who disguises his insecurity, contempt, and envy of others in wit and sarcasm. Similarly his "art," the crutch upon which he leans heavily to create a sense of self-importance and meaning, is that of caricature. The structure of his life, in other words, is dependent upon a jester's stance of detachment from and ridicule of the world. The center of that world, as far as he is concerned, is his brother Andrew, who is seemingly blessed with all the attributes he lacks: charisma, good looks, acclaim, love, success, normality. He simultaneously envies and despises his brother, whose more vivid personality has since childhood served to diminish him as a person.

When Andrew dies, he becomes obsessed with death, which he animates in the figure the "Angel of Death." Initially this Angel is coeval with Andrew, who seems to hover over and to jeer at Hugh from beyond the grave: "Andrew in my mind's eye. . . . A gigantic angel, enormous ungainly wings, brutal dark-stained muscles of stone" (p. 4). But eventually he views Andrew himself as a victim of the Angel, which has become an emblem for all the inexplicable forces beyond the control of the ego: "hideous power! . . . the Angel is sheer essence, sheer act, physicality at the point at which it is spirit" (pp. 94–95). Later, although he does not perceive the connection, his drawing of the Angel of Death takes on the features of his brother Stephen: "Dark hair, curly hair, thick hair falling upon his forehead. Angel of Death. Sexless, like a child. Neuter. Innocent. And yet so brutal" (pp. 198–99). For him, as for Andrew and Yvonne,

Stephen is an archetypal figure. But Hugh, like the others, can see this figure only negatively, as threatening to his conscious ego-control—as the Angel of Death, not the Angel of Life. In his increasingly crazed drawings, Hugh "crucifies" this figure in a "copulation-crucifixion, my personal revenge upon the Angel of Death and the Woman—the Angel crucified on a ludicrous fleshy cross—a woman's body upside down" (p. 203). The Woman is the "giantess" who haunts his dreams, the dream figure he confuses with Yvonne, whom he imagines he loves. In his increasing irrationality he imagines that he can take his brother's place in his wife's affections.

His Jungian psychiatrist, Dr. Swann, more astute than his Freudian one, is devastatingly accurate in his identification of the symbolic dimension of this anima, this female dream figure,[11] and warns Hugh against the dangers of the union he so much desires. The doctor claims that "the giantess is your own being, your own essence, slipped from your grasp—drawn back into the unconscious and now swollen, hideous, ready to devour you—ready to destroy your sanity." He cautions Hugh that he "must accept" his "own smallness, your essential triviality—a blight of the spirit." He is, in effect, an infant whose "art" is "an infant's revenge upon the adults who surround him—an infant's art work—smearing of excrement upon a world others have created." He is only half a person—"Your intelligence is everything, your emotional grasp is nothing." If he attempted now to recover the other half of his being, if symbolically he attempted sexual union with the giantess, he would be too small for her; she would destroy him. He would lose the self-deceiving rationalizations which have allowed him to cope with the world: "Your conscious being would be flooded with her, you would lose all sense of yourself, your orientation to the world." Instead, the doctor urges Hugh to live with his "impotence" (pp. 194–96).

But Hugh responds with anger, not acquiescence, to this advice. Sinking further and further into psychosis, he finally attempts suicide in a restaurant, shooting himself after he shoots the fish on his plate, which he imagines is engaged in a dialogue with him. The fish too, as Jung has pointed out repeatedly,[12] is an archetypal image of the self. Coming from the depth of the shadow world, it has attributes of God and the unconscious. Hugh's shooting of the fish thus prefigures his attempt to assassinate himself. In another sense his abortive suicide is a mad attempt to create a sense of his own importance, to stage an original scene, to astound the world with his creativity and genius, to transform the perpetual "comedy" of his life into an impressive "tragedy." Hugh is incapable of tragedy; he remains, in fact, the same pathetic, absurd, comic figure he has always been. Only retrospectively does one understand the puzzling scene that opens the book, where Hugh is depicted as a functioning brain attached to a paralyzed body in a hospital ward, a figure in a "comedy" unable to communicate with his "audience": "They have fixed my neck to a steel rod. The comedy continues. At a distance people are staring, giggling. Someone sighs. Coughs. Perhaps there is an audience. Folding chairs in the tiny cell, in the aisles between the beds, in the corridor outside. I don't know. . . . But my brain survives. It will continue. It will outlive me" (p. 3). Deprived of death or life, he is nonetheless not relieved of the burden of consciousness.

The mild, Christlike Stephen holds the key which could, although it does not, unlock the tortured egos of the other family members. He counters their intense egocentricity with extreme selflessness. In his oneness with God he is in harmony with the world of spirit, the unconscious denied or suppressed by the others. But although occasionally cognizant of his role as a potential "savior," the Petries are not saved, and Stephen himself is left bereft and unanchored to his family or his God at the end of the novel. Personally and collectively the self remains fragmented. The assassins—not at large within society but suppressed within the individual's psyche—do their bloody deeds.

Stephen is an ineffectual, strange, and at times ludicrous figure who bears rather incongruously his heavy symbolic role in the novel. Since a small child he has been a mystic, has been "one with God." His emptiness as a "frightened miniature adult, a child with no core to him," the "years in a void" (p. 449), develop a readiness for such a "fulfillment in God." This oneness with God is not a narrowly religious experience; it is, rather, a responsiveness to the unconscious self, what Jung calls the "will of God."[13] God frees Stephen from the ego, from the need to be "Stephen": "God was perpetual, permanent; 'Stephen' was of no more consequence than a fluttering leaf" (p. 517).

But Stephen's mystical dreaminess is sometimes treated humorously. He lives at a distance from his body, and at least once he has difficulty rejoining it. One day as a child at school when his teacher tries frantically to arouse him, his "nameless, wordless" being floats around at home and outside. When he attempts to reenter his body "he was rejected; it was like flinging himself at a wall. He slid against the throat, then against the soft, tender flesh where the neck joins the body, but he was repulsed, barred" (p. 499). Although he does eventually rejoin his body, obviously Stephen is no ordinary individual, since this incident is only one extreme example of the severe mind-body split which has characterized his life since childhood. Stephen, then, like the other members of his family, has found a defense against life in the flesh, against the turmoil of the emotions. It is a defense against pain, against the complicated entanglements of interpersonal relationships: *"Life in the flesh hurts,* Stephen sometimes thought. The revelation surprised him anew each time. God had no feelings, no sensations, no nerve endings. When God departed from man, pain was a possibility" (p. 524).

During long periods of his life when he is "one with God" he is placidly serene, impersonally compassionate. But when "God departs" from him as He occasionally does, Stephen is sometimes overcome by suppressed emotions. For example, one morning "at approximately ten-fifteen" God departed from Stephen, who was then caring for his special charge, a gawky, mentally disturbed child, so that Stephen is bereft of his Godlike compassion: "he was left staring at the hideously ugly face of a freakish child-giant, whom he loathed with every particle of his being" (p. 532). While Stephen is seemingly the loving and compassionate brother, Andrew sees that his impersonal love is really an abnegation of responsibility. Although sympathetic, Stephen is unable to minister to either of his brothers' needs, because he fears losing his own self-protective composure: "He was confronting Andrew Petrie, who despised him, who was a hole, a hollowness, a vacuum into which he, Stephen, might suddenly plunge and be lost—might suddenly be wrenched from the fixed state of his own being, which was complete, which was with God. He was confronting a brother, an enemy; he was confronting another human being" (p. 549). Symbolically he is the Christ figure, the image of the unified self. But as a person he is incomplete; he has abnegated the ego, a necessary component of a healthy psyche.[14]

Indeed, Andrew feels that people like himself bear the burden of consciousness so *"that people like you, Stephen, can dream virtuous dreams in which heroism is possible, in which everything works out for the glory of God"* (p. 541). Although he does not believe in Stephen's "God" he believes and fears that one can be enveloped by what Stephen calls God. He fears, in other words, the deathly stillness of egoless serenity, the "unspinning" world.

Stephen, like the others, is profoundly affected by his brother's death. Apparently Andrew was right; Stephen needed him to live in

the world of existential reality so that he could drift in his realm of
mystical oneness. Just as his brother Hugh needs Andrew to focus his
hate, so too Stephen needs him to live that life he has forfeited. While
"God" lives out Stephen's emotional life, Andrew is his ego. Stephen
has some sense of his dependence upon his brother: "that man set in
such rigid opposition to him was actually a form of himself" (p. 522).
When that part of himself dies, he no longer has the luxury of his
Godlike detachment. Like Yvonne, he is overcome with the
meaninglessness of everyone's life: "The secret was out: everyone
was doomed" (p. 561).

In a devastating dream at the end of the novel, Stephen envisions
an apocalyptic destruction of the human world by a merciless God
who orders the fowls of heaven to feast upon "the flesh of kings, and
the flesh of captains, and the flesh of mighty men, and the flesh of
horses, and of them that sit on them, and the flesh of all men, both
free and bond, both small and great" and "gather themselves unto the
supper of the Great God" (p. 566). Stephen sees the total ineffectuality of his sorrowful empathy with human beings. This God, who
ludicrously merges into a pitchman of American capitalism ("God is in
a rush. First come, first served. First in, first out. . . . Don't doubt,
don't fear. You can ask for a refund. Money back. Certainly.
Guarantee. Don't you believe me? Have faith. Faith!"), demands
detachment from Stephen: "Sorry, are you, running wild amidst the
sufferers, you who dared descend from your cloud? . . . You'll pay for
this Stephen your pretty face will pay for this the boys are going to
gang up on you and make you pay with your blood and I am sending
from all corners of the earth ferocious waters to batter you" (pp.
566–67). Upon waking, Stephen realizes "from now on, even God
must be repudiated" (p. 568). Having lost his God forever and forced
to live in the real and incomprehensible world, Stephen travels
aimlessly around the country, an accommodating perpetual "guest"
in a world of casual acquaintances.

The Petries share a common debilitating condition: all attempt
unsuccessfully half a life, a life divorced from the body. Pathetically,
each is trying to establish a meaningful, self-sustaining connection to
the world. Andrew has a utopian vision of all mankind uniting in a
common search for the truth, but he is unable to shake off recurrent
fits of depression and despair. Yvonne shares his vision in theory, but
in practice she extends the intellectual union only to her husband.
She is sustained, in fact, by envisioning the rest of the world as "the
other," The Enemy, from whom she must forever protect herself.

When she sees that "the other" is not really The Enemy but merely other people using the same words in different ways, acting out roles as they must, she loses her self-sustaining sense of isolation and uniqueness and wants only to die. Similarly, Hugh's connection to the world is dependent upon antagonism and ridicule, but when his brother dies, and his invective loses its focus, he so desperately seeks another kind of union that he loses his sanity in the attempt. Finally, Stephen's oneness with God, his responsiveness to the unconscious, is the way lost to the others—the key to individuation—but when he loses his brother he also loses his connection to the world of consciousness. He must repudiate his God, and he is left with nothing as he goes out into the world of ordinary experiences.

The connection that each seeks is broken and each is left isolated and—except for Stephen—suicidal in a seemingly meaningless world. The book is so depressing partly because there is no hope for any of the characters caught as they are in their various neuroses and psychoses. Oates argues that they are not "*especially* disturbed" and she laments the "foolish and tyrannical ideal of the 'norm' in our society that has little to do with life as it's lived."[15] But nonetheless one must insist that the Petries—a ranting psychotic, a suicidal public figure, a frigid schizoid, a drifting mystic—are not ordinary run-of-the-mill people. One could accept their eccentricities and their problems more readily if one could care about them as people; if there seemed to be some redeeming humanity about them, or some hope for them that would inspire concern and compassion. But it is hard to care about these excessively eccentric and unattractive people. This novel is, moreover, both difficult to understand and open to a wide range of interpretation. The fragmented presentation—although appropriate for the revelation of the inner lives of the characters—does not help. Oates is a skillful storyteller, a master at creating scenes, at heightening drama and tension, and at deftly sketching character. She abandons these capabilities here in the attempt to portray the play of the minds of disturbed individuals. Just as her short stories are less successful when she relies on unrelieved inner monologue, so too is this novel less skillfully rendered than others more objectively presented. All of these characters—especially that obnoxious and incessant ranter, Hugh—share a self-indulgent obsession with the same issues, scenes, and thoughts; and because their thoughts are either directly rendered or directly summarized, the reader must suffer through endless rehashing, restatement, and repetition. The ambitious scope and the intricate structural and symbolic complexity of this experimental novel are impressive, but the reader is not given enough guidance to appreciate and enjoy its emerging design.

II   Childwold: *Self and the Other*

Childwold examines much more explicitly than Oates's earlier fiction the relationship of the many and the One—transient individual egos and the continuing stream of life. Echoing and in somes senses parodying Vladimir Nabokov's *Lolita,* the action centers around a writer named Kasch's infatuation with a fourteen-year-old girl, Laney Bartlett, and his subsequent attraction and engagement to her mother, Arlene, which ends abruptly with his killing of Arlene's former lover, Earl Tuller. But the thematic center of the book resides in the various characters' attempts to come to terms with the continuities and discontinuities of personality, the junctures and the connections between the self and "the other": family, other people, nature.

Son of a prominent family, Fitz John Kasch has led a seemingly successful life first as an outstanding student and then as published writer of several books. Having been married and divorced, he now at forty deliberately rejects his former self in an attempted ascetic retreat into the country of his childhood. Equipped with the writings of "Meister Eckhart, of Pascal, of Shakespeare, of Boehme, of Saint Augustine, of Thoreau, of Kierkegaard, of Rilke, and Nietzsche and Santayana; the Upanishads, the Bible, the Tibetan Book of the Dead," he attempts to examine and to redirect his life, to shed all that is artificial and false, to transcend through ascetic denial the disconnected fragments of his life, and to achieve a mystical identification with the One (p. 127).[16] But from the beginning he is incapable of sustaining his quest. At the point of despair, he is suicidal and sadistic, even fantasizing the murder of a child. Wandering aimlessly one evening, he chances to see some boys taunting and seemingly torturing a young girl. Rushing to her rescue, he is struck with the angelic beauty of this girl, Laney Bartlett. His subsequent relationship with her draws Kasch back into life, pulling him away from his attempted asceticism. This "angel," this "Lilith," whom he simultaneously adores and ravages, to whom he responds as both daughter and lover, is for him a figure of enchantment in spite of his intellectual rejection of her: "I hate Laney's smoke-stinking clothes, her premature cynicism, her slight, almost dwarfish figure. I hate her fate—her doom. I am not involved with it or with her" (p. 126). Like Humbert Humbert's nymphet, Lolita, Kasch's Laney is in some sense a figment of his imagination whom he pretends he can obliterate ("Laney, do you doubt me? If you doubt me you will cease to exist!" [p. 109]) or "transform" at will: "I will invent her. I will write about her with devotion, abstracting from her certain qualities I find poignant and eliminating others I find vulgar" (p. 111). But Laney's separate selfhood, like Lolita's, must be recognized at last: "You are no longer recognizable! You are no longer mine!" (p. 290). While this relationship opens Kasch up to emotional experience, it is frustratingly unliberating: "I am miserable with affection that cannot be discharged." He remains locked in his schizoid disunity: "There is no God. I am not filled with God. I am pure consciousness trapped in time, in a body, I am unenlightened, I am dragged in a circle, I am helpless to fight free" (p. 126).

When he meets Arlene, Laney's mother, however, he feels joyfully reborn. Laney was apparently just a portent of the mother, who functions, it seems, as the Great Mother archetype for Kasch's impoverished unconscious. Arlene is portrayed as a woman at home in her body and in the world. Loving sexual experience and pregnancy, she presides over a brood of children from various fathers, the slatternly center of a crowded household on a ramshackle farm teeming with fecundity. Her almost mindless grounding within the "real" world, within instinctual, physical experience, is the antithesis of Kasch's overdeveloped intellectuality; and in his wholehearted embrace of her and her life he feels momentarily the oneness and unity which eluded him through asceticism: "You hold them all in one embrace. All. Always. Forever. I love—. . . They are yours. They are you" (pp. 268–69). He feels like a child awakened to a new joyful existence: "I am new, I am trembling with newness, I am like a child, I am innocent of past accomplishments as well as past sins, there is no connection, no attachment, I cast such things from me, reckless with the joy of . . . reckless with joy" (p. 253).

Kasch feels at this point that there is no necessary and inevitable continuity of the human personality, that he can start his life all over again on an entirely different plane. But he is apparently mistaken. In a passage reverberating with symbolic overtones, Arlene is portrayed as a powerful earth goddess giving her lover the kiss of death, as it were, the seed from the tree of death, the yew: "The woman laugh Filled to the brim, she is, plump-breasted, her belly compact, her hips and thighs strong, her legs strong, firm, taut. My love! Lips

moist, parted in a sly smile, between her teeth a seed, is it?—a tiny
seed—a yew seed—you step forward and, trembling, bring your
mouth to hers, your eager mouth to hers, you kiss, you taste, you eat:
a tiny seed from a yew cone" (p. 268). Foreshadowed in this passage is
the sacrifice which Kasch will make for Arlene. Later defending her,
he kills her former lover, Earl Tuller. Tuller, a zesty, volatile, simple
man of action, is Kasch's alter ego, the man whom he cannot change
into, however much he would like to invent himself anew on a simple,
physical level. After a trial and a period in a mental hospital, Kasch
claims he is "dead," living like a hermit on the abandoned farm of the
Bartlett's.

Laney senses a spiritual affinity with Kasch, for she too suffers from
her own kind of schizoid self. Playing the role of the teenage tart, she
belongs to the wild, fast, disreputable high-school crowd, yet this
hard exterior masks a sensitive and intelligent young girl, fearful of
experience, anxious about her family, yearning for connection and
fulfillment. When under stress she is capable of severe mind-body
split as evidenced by her total departure from her body when as a
child she was in danger of drowning. After she was rescued by her
brother Vale, she told her mother that she "had died, had gone to a
new place. Not just going to sleep, but to a new place. In the water
. . . there was water in my mouth and my eyes but I was outside the
water too, watching" (p. 76). She has one moment of mystical
identification with her body and with nature. When experiencing
menstruation as a young girl, she feels life streaming through her and
around her without her conscious control: "you must float with the
current, the plunge of the rapids, you must close your eyes and move
with it, everything is spilling toward you, around you, inside you,
through you, your blood flows with it, you are rivers and streams and
creeks, there is a heartbeat inside you, around you—" (p. 197). But
this experience is unique. While her relationship with Kasch awakens
her intellectually so that she, the child of an impoverished family,
develops an avid desire for knowledge and culture, she is not able to
respond to him sexually. Thinking of her mother's sexual responsiveness ("God I love it. I can't get enough of it"), she feels only panic and
despair: "you can't respond, you freeze and want to push him away"
(p. 154). When she reaches the point of thinking that she does love
Kasch, he is asleep and the moment passes forever: "you aren't going
to see him again, you are greatly relieved, you are sick with the loss,
you are triumphant" (p. 217). Permanently changed through her
relationship with Kasch, Laney is yet unfulfilled.

Laney's brother, Vale, suffers the most extreme discontinuity of selfhood of all. Severely wounded in Vietnam, he no longer looks, acts, or thinks like his former self. Maimed physically and psychologically, he pathetically tells himself that he is perfectly well, drifting about committing mindless crimes and aggressive acts, cut off from his family, yet drawn to them by complex emotional bonds. His tragedy is his dulled perception, coupled with his sadistic brutality. He too is "dead"—his former self died, like Kasch's, in a clash with an enemy. His spirit, too, had been questing for unity with the female principle; but he is destroyed through the terrible waste of the Vietnam War: "—his penis hardened, shaftlike, helpless to stop what was happening!—his life, the living kernel of him, fled violently through him and into the mud and was gone. No sensation, no ecstasy: only a groaning whimpering threshing struggle. It wanted freedom from his dying body, it wanted to mate with and impregnate the earth" (p. 258). For Vale the problems of selfhood are compounded by horrible conditions imposed by society, chance, and circumstance.

Joseph Hurley, Laney and Vale's eighty-three-year-old grandfather, is especially sensitive to the discontinuities of the personal life, the dimming of the significance of events with the passing of years, and the omnipotence of Nature over the mere human. Thinking of the young, caught up as they are in the particulars of their lives, he asks exasperatedly: "don't they know the heat-haze will settle over them, the hills will be alive with white and yellow and orange-and-black butterflies, their shouts will be drowned out by the insects' droning and singing, don't they know, don't you know—?" (p. 47). While Joseph Hurley has suffered through some painful experiences in his life—a separation from his mother and father at an early age when he was sent to America to live with his uncle, a marriage to an unhappy and unexpressive woman, an unrequited love affair—he still feels a satisfying bond of oneness to the land that he works and to Nature, which calls to him with increasing insistence in his old age. He does not wish to be stripped of his dignity and consciousness like his alter ego, Josef Krassov, who mindlessly clings to life in a nursing home; rather, he is drawn inexorably to the river he has dreamt about which obliterates all that is temporal and unites him in death to the land and the girl he loves:

Those vivid dreams last night still with me: the farmland so bright, glowing, as if on fire with invisible flames. Such heat, such radiance. . . . The attic window beneath the peak of the roof illuminated, glowing, glaring, my darling, my Pearl, my sweet frightened girl in the window. . . . The dream-river crashing and plunging at my feet. . . . Seeping into my shoes: so cold! A sign, a sign? My heart swelling with joy . . . with dread . . . with joy. . . . Many-pulsed, tumultuous. (p. 254)

Joseph walks to his death in the river, an event which saddens his family, especially his daughter Arlene, but which is presented in the novel as a joyful acceptance of death as an intrinsic part of life. Indeed, Josph has had intimations of life beyond death. He ponders the curious phenomenon of the returning "presence" of his wife's young cousin Lenny, killed in the first world war; he urges his dead lover Pearl to come closer to him. Furthermore, his grandchildren swear that he himself returns to their house after his death "trying to tell them something." Through his inarticulate mysticism, Joseph occasionally experiences a kind of oneness with the life force that eludes most of the other characters of the novel except his daughter Arlene who seems to be the very embodiment of it.

Arlene is the type of woman Oates has portrayed before. Reminiscent of Clara of *A Garden*, Loretta of *them*, Ardis of *Do With Me*, she is a more positive character. Like the others, she is rather vulgar, foul-mouthed, and selfish, but she is a healthier animal than they are—a woman who enjoys her own sexuality, who is firmly footed in physical and emotional experience, a likable, warm-hearted character who has none of the neuroses of her daughter Laney. But she does not have Laney's sensitivities and intelligence either. Limited in her capacities to evaluate experience, Arlene is the happiest character in the novel, carrying on zestfully when others fail. Indeed, her life is strewn with the literal or figurative deaths of her men: her husband, Lyle Bartlett, killed in an auto accident and her lover, Earl Tuller, killed by her fiancé, Fitz John Kasch, who himself suffers another kind of death. At the end of the novel she has yet another lover, Wally, and in spite of the recent tragic events—the deaths of her father and Tuller, the trial and sentencing of Kasch—she is out having a good time at a picnic. At times larger than life, she is the Great Mother who inspires allegiance and sacrifice from her lovers, who devours as well as nurtures, who uses men in an almost impersonal gratification of her sexual and procreative drives.

The kind of elemental harmony that Arlene possesses, the open responsiveness to her physical being, is not a state which could be easily achieved by others. Kasch, smitten by and longing for all that

Arlene represents, cannot duplicate her simplicity, cannot achieve her harmony; he is doomed by his attraction to what he cannot be. Similarly, Laney feels intimidated and dwarfed by her mother's comfortable physicality. Both of these characters who have active mental lives are not at home in the physical world and suffer from feelings of disconnectedness. Yet for these people perhaps the only authentic life is the inner one. Indeed at a moment of lucidity, Kasch recognizes the essential falsity of the life of outward action to which he is drawn:

The interior life constitutes the authentic life, and actions performed in the exterior world are peripheral. Reality is what I am thinking, what is thinking through me, using me as a means, a vessel, a reed, even, streaming through with or without my consent; the interior life is continuous, unhurried, almost undirected, unheralded. Flow of thoughts, feelings, emotions, observations. Broken reflections. The glittering, winking look of the river. Surely our outward gestures are misleading, surely our deepest selves are mocked even by our good deeds, our charity. The sinister "self" that is photographed. Frozen in one attitude. A lie. (p. 138)

Similarly, Laney is impressed with the "powerful directed flow not to be stopped, not to be stopped for long" (p. 239) that life is. Elusive fulfillment seems to reside in the characters' fitful ability to identify selflessly with this flow.

Earlier Kasch did achieve an occasional moment of transcendence through asceticism: "a few minutes' genuine pleasure in attaining a kind of purity of consciousness—a break-through, as if to another level of being—but only temporary, only temporary" (p. 134). He regrets furthermore his impulsive defense of Arlene: "The stupidity of brute action: a corresponding stupidity in the body, in the very marrow of the bones. Futility. Waste. They are right, they are right, the saints who teach contemplation, who shy away from action! They are right!" (p. 290). By withdrawing the narrative from Kasch's consciousness at the end of the novel, Oates leaves his future rather ambiguous. Perhaps he can now pursue his asceticism freed from the distracting enchantment of the physical world, although he does appear to be an embittered, broken man.

Similarly, the final view of Laney is somewhat confusing. Kasch thinks of her as coming to a consciousness beyond his: "You stir, you wake, you come to consciousness, heaved upon the sands of consciousness; but where are you, why have you gone so far? The books you read are not my books, the language you use is not my language"

(p. 290). Indeed, having moved from her mother's house, Laney begins to read intensively, distancing herself from her origins; but the novel ends with her standing outside of Kasch's retreat, awaiting some "sign" from him. While contentment, peace, unity seem to elude these two characters, their future remains unknown.

The book does not offer ready and simplistic answers to the questions it raises about the individual self in relationship to the other; the problem of relatedness is experienced by different characters in different ways. Those who are contemplative and rational have a more difficult time than the more intuitive and emotional characters. Yet the novel records some beautiful momentary experiences of transcendence of self. Often the continuity of life outside of ego-consciousness is depicted imagistically as flowing riverlike: Laney experiences it as life pulsing within and around her during menstruation; Kasch, through the undirected, continuous stream of the inner life and through his loving identification with Arlene's family; Joseph Hurley, through the dream river blending past and present and merging with the actual river into which he plunges, and through his intimations of an existence transcending even death; Arlene, through sexual orgasm and joyful pregnancies. In many ways the most satisfying of Oates's novels, *Childwold* is set in the Eden County of her early fiction. Oates evokes this world and its people with warmth, compassion, and authenticity. Furthermore, she uses here a technique very well suited to her subject. Grounding the novel in the consciousness of her characters, she moves back and forth from one to another, effectively reinforcing the sense of isolation, yet relatedness, of these individuals. Not only is the novel ordered lyrically rather than narratively but the language itself is lyrical, possessing often a poetic quality rare in Oates's novels.

I regret that I do not have the space here to give the complex styles of both *The Assassins* and *Childwold* the attention they deserve. The experimental nature of these novels suggests that Oates is moving away from the conventional narrative style which has dominated much of her work. One hopes that she will learn to combine this method with greater clarity of presentation. Ambitious and interesting as these two novels are, the reader wishes for more guidance in evaluation of character and action.

CHAPTER 6

The Short Stories:
The Experimental Ground

H AVING by 1977 published ten collections and scores of uncollected short stories, Joyce Carol Oates is one of the most prolific and masterful contributors to the genre writing today. While the same thematic concerns are manifest in all of her fiction, she has used the short story with greater flexibility than the novel. The short story has provided the experimental ground that attests to her continual exploration and growth as a writer. She has, for example, written Joycean short stories which build up dramatic tensions to a final epiphany. She has experimented extensively with variations on the interior monologue. She has created innumerable images of "Kali," the dark half of female totality. She has written academic satires, rewritten short-story masterpieces of other writers, even "translated" stories by an imaginary Portuguese author. While many of her stories display a precision, control, and thematic luminosity that assure them a secure place among the finest stories of our language, some of her experimental stories are undistinguished. *The Wheel of Love*, most frequently mentioned as her best short-story collection, offers the opportunity to examine the artistic vicissitudes of this versatile short-story writer.

I   The Wheel of Love: *Uneven Craftsmanship*

The Wheel of Love, like so many of Oates's collections, is thematically unified. Focusing exclusively on the emotional complexity of human relationships, the collection offers a rich—if distressing— view of the mysterious, volatile, and disorienting power of love. Commonly, Oates depicts a character seeking release from the "strain and risk" of love (p. 7).[1] The woman of "Unmailed, Unwritten Letters" imagines her lover's violent death and listlessly attempts to

effect her own by pressing her wrist against the jagged and rusty edge
of a tin can. Another story begins: "I was in love with a man I couldn't
marry, so one of us had to die—I lay awake, my eyes twitching in the
dark, trying to understand which one of us should die" (p. 337). Nadia
of "The Wheel of Love," trapped in the claustrophobia of her
husband's love, commits suicide. Nina of "The Heavy Sorrow of the
Body" finds an equally extreme expedient: she takes on the identity of
a male, since "men had a kind of anonymity she desired; they were
negations most of them. . . . She wanted to draw into herself the
terrible experiences of her life—the violence of her love for men, the
violence of her fear of them—and, in herself, bring them to nothing"
(p. 290).

These women, caught in the maelstrom of love, are at least capable
of feeling. Yet *The Wheel of Love* is populated with innumerable men
and women who have sealed themselves off from physical and
emotional experience. Oates often employs religious figures like
Sister Irene of "In the Region of Ice" and Father Rollins of "Shame" to
depict the emotional sterility that sometimes accompanies the protective sanctuary of the celibate life. Other characters do not need the
garb of the religious life to exclude physically. Pauline of "Bodies," a
talented sculptress interested only in "heads," for example, is coolly
aloof from "bodies," from the physical and emotional bonds among
people, until an emotionally disturbed young man forces her into a
relationship by the violent expedient of slashing his throat before her
on the street. Emotionally sterile individuals sometimes imitate the
seeming normality of others. Dorie, the impressionable young
college girl of "Accomplished Desires," infatuated with her professor, his wife, and their life, succeeds in literally moving in and
supplanting the wife after she conveniently commits suicide, but
despite her "accomplished desires" Dorie is unable to overcome her
daydreaming vacuousness: "she was this girl sitting at a battered desk
in someone's attic, and no one else, no other person . . . she was
herself and that was a fact, a final fact she would never overcome" (p.
310). David of "Convalescing," eager to be judged normal, tries to
anticipate the expected responses to a public opinion questionnaire
and clings to his vivacious wife for the strength and identity he
personally lacks.

A number of Oatesian characters are so entangled in filial relationships that they are incapable of healthy love relationships outside of
the family. The problems of Marion of "You" are compounded by the
fact that she shares the meager love, attention, and cast-off boyfriends

of her voluptuous movie-star mother with another slender twin. Similarly, the acne-faced adolescent of "Boy and Girl" is diminished by his father's success and good looks and by his mother's disappointment in him. Sometimes the child is alienated by the world of his parents like the girl of "How I Contemplated the World from the Detroit House of Correction," but despite her rebellion, which includes stealing and living with a junkie, she is, in the end, overpowered by her influential, affluent parents and returned to the sterile sanctuary of their world. Several of the characters are locked into a role of responsibility for an aged parent ("The Assailant," "Demons," "Matter and Energy") and freed only when a lover acts out a Freudian drama and literally assaults the tyrannizing father, as the lovers in both "The Assailant" and "Demons" do.

Feeling themselves to be either unworthy of love, unable to risk or experience it, or unhappy within it, the characters of the collection offer jointly a dismal view of the human being's incapacity to enjoy a healthy and wholesome emotional life. The pervasive low resiliency of the characters may fatigue and depress the reader as well; and the volume as a whole may leave one with an overwhelming pessimism about people's potential for fulfilling human relationships. Indeed, I think readers are put off by what strikes them at first reading as a repetitive sameness, so that they are not disposed to observe the unique craftsmanship of the individual stories and the richness and complexity with which similar themes are treated in the better stories.

The least successful kind of story, in my opinion, is usually an unrelieved interior monologue, usually related in first person, in which an emotionally distraught person dwells obsessively upon his unhappiness. Although these stories are often innovative in technique, the cleverness of conception does not compensate for a monotony of content. One such story—a favorite of Oates herself—is "Unmailed, Unwritten Letters," in which a young woman caught miserably in the throes of love composes imaginary letters to her lover, his child, her husband, and her parents as a kind of self-therapy to cope with feelings that cannot be openly expressed to these people. The device of such communications serves to introduce specific information into the story and to recapitulate pertinent background about the monologuist's marriage and her affair, while it simultaneously records her immediate responses to the people and events which shape her life. The final eight pages of the story re-create in detail, in the guise of an extended imaginary letter to her husband,

the last hours of her most recent rendezvous with her lover. But the
staccato-like report of this driven woman is awkward, monotonous,
and annoying. Her attempt to contain her near-hysteria within the
short sentences of her exhaustively thorough confession is psychologically valid, but the story does not build in dramatic intensity because
of the monotonous bombardment of every detail of action and feeling.

A more conventionally told story, "I Was in Love," is an exquisitely
tedious account of the state of high tension, guilt, and suppressed
hysteria of a woman who is having an adulterous affair. It reaches a
climax with the attempted, perhaps successful, suicide of the woman's son, who jumps out of the car in protest over the look of sexual
satiety his mother is unable to remove from her face. Oates has
attempted to prepare for this event by the child's unrest earlier.
Nonetheless, how is the reader to take this conclusion? That love is
burdensome, inconvenient, disruptive, and destructive is blatantly
clear, but should one accept this woman's misery as the inevitable
consequence of love, or does Oates mean to isolate specific traits of
this woman which create her suffering? Oates has failed to give her
story a meaningful shape. Like the woman herself, the reader
achieves no perspective on her situation; there's no illumination, no
epiphany, no climax beyond the contrived death of her son.

Some stories fail for just the opposite reason: the specific situation
rendered fails to support the ponderous generalization affixed to it.
Such a story is "What Is the Connection Between Men and
Women?"—a rhetorical question that is not, in my reading, satisfactorily answered. This story is punctuated by italicized questions
posed apparently by the omniscient narrator to heighten the restless
insomnia and the mounting tension of an aggrieved widow who is the
focus of the story. A man with a striking resemblance to her husband
follows her, telephones her, and apparently pursues her to the door of
her apartment. At the end of the story, "she reaches up to slide the
little bolt back and everything comes open, comes apart" (p. 383).
Here is the climactic epiphany in which the disparate pieces of the
story come together? Perhaps, but what has happened? Has her
husband revisited her from the grave? Has she been engaged in a
compelling fantasy dream which "comes apart" when she opens the
door? Is a stranger about to assault her sexually? At the alleged
moment of illumination, all remains dark. What *is* the connection
between men and women? Surely the story does not show or tell. At
the very most it attempts to show the connection between an
intensely overwrought woman and an enigmatic pursuer, a connec-

tion that is vague, unrealized, and important only to the imagination; but it is impossible to conclude that their "connection," whatever it is, exemplifies *the* connection between men and women. *"How does it feel to be a woman?"* Surely not like this "answer" to the ponderous question: "Eyeballs: dense white balls of matter. Skin: stretched tight and hot across the bones" (p. 382). This woman and man fail to achieve universality, just as the conclusion of the story fails to be illuminating.

If Joyce Carol Oates wrote only stories like these or others (one could mention "Matter and Energy," "The Assailant," "Wild Saturday," and "An Interior Monologue") her work would be disappointing. Fortunately, however, she has written many perfect or near-perfect stories which bear only a thematic resemblance to these. Her most successful vantage point is at a distance from her characters where she can dispassionately sketch with deft strokes their interior and exterior lives, place them in vividly specific contexts, and clinically record the mounting tensions and conflicts of the story. Two of the most memorable stories of this collection—"In the Region of Ice" and "Where Are You Going, Where Have You Been?"—display Oates's scalpellike control of the tools of her trade. Both begin with a sketch of the central character which suggests through a few descriptive details qualities of disposition which will function importantly in the story: the imposing illusion of intelligence, seriousness, and restraint of Sister Irene; the shallow, adolescent narcissism of Connie. Oates introduces early in each story the man who will generate the tension. Sister Irene is challenged in class by the probing query of a visiting student; Connie notices at a shopping plaza the man who later shows up at her place.

Oates brilliantly re-creates the plastic world of shopping centers and fly-specked drive-in restaurants which serve as the adolescent haven and stalking ground in "Where Are You Going." Connie, bathed in "trashy daydreams" and in the sentimental lyrics of popular songs and prompted by vague stirrings of sexual consciousness, experiments with provocation, tried on like cheap makeup, when she is beyond the suspicious eye of her mother; "She wore a pull-over jersey blouse that looked one way when she was at home and another way when she was away from home. Everything about her had two sides to it, one for home and one for anywhere that was not home" (p. 30).

The tension is incrementally heightened through Connie's gradual awakening to the nature and intent of the young man, Arnold Friend, who shows up at her house while her family is away. At first puzzled and flattered by his attention, she is coolly and coyly flirtatious. But she observes without recognizing their significance some anomalies such as the year-old slang expression on Friend's car and his failure to "come together" into a credible image in spite of his mod gear and his popularized, predictable speech and manner. Then, shockingly, Friend's much older self begins to emerge through his painted lashes, black wig, reflecting sunglasses, and cosmetically tanned face—when his telltale, aging throat is inadvertently exposed. Connie's terror reaches such a height that she is immobilized, screaming hopelessly into the dial tone of the telephone. At the end of the story, she is moved off unresistingly by her creepy seducer, whose formulaic sing-song words, "My sweet little blue-eyed girl," complete the mockery of brown-eyed Connie's adolescent dream world.

The story is enriched by the very ordinariness of Connie and her friends and their dreamy infatuation with the sleazy and experimental no-man's-land of adolescence. Connie's encounter with Arnold Friend is not just a unique instance of how one girl's experimental flirtation propels her too rapidly into the world of experience, not just an account of one girl's perception of the deceptiveness of appearances and the terrible reality of evil, but a particularly vivid instance of a universal experience: the loss of innocence. Indeed, Oates plays up the representational quality of the experience by inviting the reader to see Arnold Friend as the Arch Fiend, the Devil-in-disguise.[2]

While Connie is hopelessly initiated into evil, Sister Irene successfully retreats into the region of ice, a protective state of innocent noninvolvement, but not without irreparable damage to both Allen Weinstein, the brilliant and disturbed student who appeals to her for emotional and intellectual communion, and herself. A much different kind of story, "In the Region of Ice" is developed not through the rich and suggestive descriptive detail of "Where Are You Going" but through an exact recording of Sister Irene's feelings toward Weinstein. She is stimulated by his presence in class, hurt when he is absent, simultaneously responsive and chilled by his appeals for sympathy, hurt and confused when he appears indifferent, protective when he seems vulnerable. But most dominant is her terror at becoming involved: "She was terrified at what he was trying to do—he was trying to force her into a human relationship" (p. 18). But against her will she is drawn to him, and ironically she, a nun, feels that for the first time "she was being forced into the role of a Christian, and what did that mean?" (p. 19).

In response to his letter from a mental sanitorium, she appeals to his parents to bring him home, an extraordinary gesture of concern from this restrained and inhibited woman. But later, when Weinstein again visits her at her office and tries to initiate a personal relationship, she backs out of involvement, resuming the mask of nun and professor. He drops out of her life; she returns to the regularity and anonymity of her teaching career. Later, hearing of his suicide, "she could not really regret Weinstein's suffering and death; she had only one life and had already given it to someone else. He had come too late to her" (pp. 27–28). Presumably the someone else is God, to whom she has made her religious vows, but those vows did not include a negation of all human relationships. Obviously, she is restricted not by her vocation, but by her emotional timidity and frigidity. She has failed both Weinstein and herself in this choice of the "region of ice."[3]

What makes "In the Region of Ice" and "Where Are You Going" so memorable is not only the precise rendering of the central character's evolving response to the male intruder in her world, but also the richness and clarity of thematic statement. Sister Irene is one of many frigid, inhibited women in Oates's fiction, but unlike many of them, she is portrayed as a person at least partially responsible for her own limitations. Offered the chance for redemption, for human communion, she chooses to remain isolated and alone. Of course, one should not underestimate the difficulty of the situation for her—this anguish is what makes the story so richly complex—but the reader does not go away from the story as he does from the lesser ones with an overwhelming sense of hopelessness about the potentiality of all human relationships. This particular one failed because Sister Irene lacked the courage to participate in it, not because all are doomed to be ineffectual and miserable. Because the reader understands her personal failure as she does not, he is not locked in the same hopelessness as she is.

Similarly, "Where Are You Going" is more than a tale of the inevitable seduction of a young girl like Connie. Oates captures so well the vacuousness, cheapness, and narcissism of the life of Connie and her friends who have nothing better to do than to stroll up and down a shopping-center plaza looking for excitement. The implications of the title are that Connie has not been asked, "Where are you going, where have you been?" with any rigor by her nagging mother and her indifferent father. Left to her own amusements, she plays dangerously with a sexuality she poorly understands, as she unconsciously invites her seduction out of a misguided desire for attention. Again, the reader can rise above the character's predicament and is, therefore, illuminated rather than depressed. Oates has given her story a meaningful shape as well as rendering it vividly. These two stories are not unique achievements in this volume or in Oates's canon. Repeatedly, she demonstrates her skill as a short-story craftsman. Others particularly noteworthy in this collection are "Accomplished Desires," "Convalescing," and "You."

This collection demonstrates that Joyce Carol Oates's province as a writer is psychological realism: the drama of her work is played out within the psyches and through the emotions of her characters. Her writing is indeed about "the mystery of human emotions," but the successful story must not leave the reader mystified as well. She has written some stories that do not permit the reader to rise above the emotional duress of the characters—stories, often first-person narratives, of unrelieved and tedious misery better told to a psychiatrist than to a reader. Occasionally Oates makes first-person narration work. She even employs second-person in "You," an effectively crafted account of a daughter's obsession with her mother. She is more often successful, however, with the built-in restraints of third-person narration. Its distancing allows her to set up characters and scenes dispassionately. The carefully chosen details, the directly rendered action, the heightening tension, and the coolly incisive authorial descriptions of feelings replace the unrelieved harangue of an emotionally distraught character and contribute to a sense of detachment and perspective.

While for many readers Oates focuses too frequently upon disturbed individuals, her most successful stories often have to do with ordinary people, people who live with a minimum of violence and hysteria, people who have achieved some modicum of adjustment to life. She is devastating at showing just what adjustments entail, such as the invitation to sexual assault behind the adolescent flirtation of Connie and the horror of emotional commitment behind the religious vows of Sister Irene. She creates these vivid portraits with the precision and craftsmanship that place her among America's major short-story writers. Another volume which contributes immeasurably to her achievement is *The Goddess and Other Women*.

II The Goddess and Other Women: *Unliberated Women*

While men have most often held center stage in Oates's novels, portraits of women predominate in Joyce Carol Oates's short stories. Only in *The Goddess and Other Women,* however, does she focus exclusively upon women. Jointly these twenty-five stories offer a composite view of women that is probing but disturbing because nearly all the principal characters are images of the Hindu goddess Kali, the dark half of the female totality.[4] Kali appears in the volume as the garish red-and-yellow statuette in the story "The Goddess," "her savage fat-cheeked face fixed in a grin, her many arms outspread, and around her neck what looked like a necklace of skulls" (pp. 407–408).[5] The skulls are symbolic of Kali's destructiveness; she is often depicted as feeding on the entrails of her lovers. But for all her terribleness, Kali is yet looked upon not as evil but as part of nature's totality: life feeds on life; destruction is an intrinsic part of nature's procreative process. So, rather than portraying women as our literary myths would have them—which, as Leslie Fiedler and others have pointed out, almost invariably depict women as either good or evil—Oates presents them as locked into the destructive form of Kali, unliberated into the totality of female selfhood.

Some of the stories in *Goddess* depict preteens toying exploitatively and dangerously with a sexuality which they do not really understand. Betsy of "Blindfold" and Nancy of "Small Avalanches" are young girls who sexually taunt considerably older men. To be sure, the men are culpable. Betsy's uncle has devised the perverse little game of blindfold, and sexual molestation is the aim of the pursuer in "Small Avalanches." But Betsy and Nancy adopt with facility the mask of feigned innocence and deliberate naiveté. Betsy accepts the private game of blindfold in exchange for her privileged position as favored niece until their game is discovered by a stranger. Then she totally abnegates all responsibility. She cruelly relishes her uncle's death and exposes his weakness to her mother. At a very young age Betsy is learning the exploitative possibilities of sexual attraction. Similarly, Nancy of "Small Avalanches" also enjoys her superior role in the sexual game she finds herself engaged in with the man who follows her in a car and then on foot. Interpreting his pursuit as a childlike game of chase, she giggles and pretends to be ignorant of his aim. When he is overcome by fatigue and heart palpitations, she like Betsy cruelly denies any responsibility: "This will teach you a lesson, I thought" (p. 239). She is a young girl learning that sex is an exciting and dangerous game where "winning" is leading on the male and then frustrating him.

A number of Oates's stories in *Goddess* and elsewhere depict a teenage girl on the brink of existential self-definition, as a "good" girl or "bad," as mother's and father's daughter or as an anonymous pick-up. Oates captures very well that point in adolescence when a girl begins to be aware of herself sexually, when she makes tentative gropings out to the world beyond childhood. "The Voyage to Rosewood," for example, depicts a sixteen-year-old, Marsha, who, bored with high school, decides to take a bus ride to another town, anywhere different. Her adventure ends with a beating by a weird young man, Ike, who had picked her up. At the end of the story her father comes to the police station to take her home. This time she is returned to the parents whom she loves and the world that is familiar, but life is experimental and identity is fluid for a young girl like Marsha, who out of boredom half-consciously wills her own molestation.

Resilient, daring, and increasingly self-sufficient, Betsy, Nancy, and Marsha approach life experimentally and men exploitatively. In some ways more distressing are the many portrayals in this volume of girls and women who are passive, frightened, withdrawn, and unfree. In spite of their inhibition, they are yet capable of unpredictable, violent behavior. They are sometimes the perpetrators, more often the victims of brutal assault.

Sarah of "In the Warehouse" is a small, skinny, insecure twelve-year-old who is totally dominated by her taller, bigger, and extremely abrasive girl friend, Ronnie. Here Oates is depicting one of these inseparable adolescent relationships, but Sarah is suffering in her unwilling bondage to Ronnie. She plans and executes a brutal escape: she pushes her friend down the stairs of an abandoned warehouse, closing off the cries for help of the dying Ronnie. In murdering Ronnie, Sarah is killing off the frightening and unwanted part of herself and the world. Twenty years later, married with two children, living in a colonial house in a comfortable suburban neighborhood, she tries but is unable to feel guilt for what she did: "There is a great shadowy space about me, filled with waiting: waiting to cry, to feel sorry. . . . But nothing happens" (p. 80). In destroying Ronnie, Sarah has destroyed her own emotional life. Through her desperate act she has secured a kind of liberation and security, but at a permanent cost to herself as a person. She has made a typical bargain of an Oatesian woman. Like Maureen Wendall of *them*, she has paid dearly for immunity.

Frequently, however, these vacuous Oatesian women become disenchanted with their emptiness and reach out for some confirmation of their being. The girl of "The Girl" is a case in point. Beautiful and bland, the girl eagerly plays The Girl in the makeshift movie of The Director. Even though the action includes a brutal and unannounced assault and rape and the girl is hospitalized as a result, she holds no resentment toward the sadistic director. Seeing him several months later, her only concern is to be assured that there was film in the camera. Pathetically she needs the film to confirm her identity as The Girl, since she has no selfhood as a particular girl.

Oates is aware of the unlimited capacity for self-abnegation and the dedication to men of some women. In "A Premature Autobiography," a young girl who is a gifted composer has a brief affair with her one-time mentor, the famous composer Bruer, and then settles for the unchallenging and mundane life of a piano teacher in a teachers' college. Yet when Bruer's autobiography comes out and she is mentioned in one paragraph as a now faceless and nameless girl who Bruer says was talented and devoted to him and to whom "in a way he owes all the work he accomplished at this time (and after this time)" (p. 382), she feels completed and confirmed as a person. Feeling no need now for any further living, she happily embraces her fixed identity as the anonymous woman-behind-the-man.

Often the frustration of women is turned inward in a conscious or unconscious quest for death. So often for Oates's women freedom seems to lie in the deadening of emotion, in the deliberate quest for nothingness. The woman of "& Answers" has so little self-esteem and so completely disparages women as people that she has attempted to kill her daughter and herself. The story consists entirely of answers to apparent questions put to her by a psychiatrist in therapy following her car accident in which her daughter Linda was killed. High-school tests indicate that she is an extraordinarily intelligent individual, but she insists that she is perfectly ordinary, average, and uninteresting. Having mastered the art of female self-deprecation, she is embarrassed by the psychiatrist's attention and theories. She has an exaggerated respect for men's opinions—all men: "I believe anything men tell me and I always did" (p. 160). But she thinks that "men expect too much" of women, expect "something like God," and women are doomed to disappoint them because they simply are not equal to these expectations. Unknowingly, this mother tried to undo her motherhood because her daughter reminded her too much of herself; and she could not bear the thought that her daughter would endure similar emptiness, fearfulness, and anxiety. Oates presents here an extraordinarily painful portrait of a woman whose wholehearted acceptance of male superiority carries with it a total denigration of herself as a woman.

Not all of Oates's women sit on the brink of suicide or madness, listlessly waiting for something to happen. Some of her most effective stories depict women with successful careers whose professional competence unfortunately is not matched by a similar facility to relate comfortably and wholesomely to men. For example, Jenny, the bright intern of "Psychiatric Services," manipulated by her clever patient, becomes entangled in various sexual roles and loses control of therapy. By taking away the gun of her patient she unwittingly plays the role of virgin castrator and confirms his suicidal tendencies and by listening to his late-night telephone conversations she falls into a pattern of love-play detrimental to their professional relationship. Meanwhile, she plays the dependent daughter to the fatherlike authority of her superior, Dr. Culloch, who belittles her by sarcastically pointing out how Jenny's feminine responses undermine her role as a professional.

The professionalism of Katherine, the social worker of "Waiting," increases as her emotional responsiveness wanes. She evolves from the eager, concerned girl who takes home the files of her welfare clients and cries over them at night to the efficient case-work supervisor who noses out fraud and cold-bloodedly enforces welfare regulations. Katherine's personal life undergoes a corresponding change. Pleading that she must care for her invalid mother, she postpones her wedding until her engagement disintegrates and gradually her life settles into an empty routine. Oates incisively yet sympathetically portrays the encroaching narrowness of the life of this woman who closes off her emotions without ever consciously making a decision to do so. The climax of the story comes when Mr. Mott, a former welfare client, encounters her on the street and gives her a ride home. After she invites him in and makes an awkward attempt to play the role of a woman hosting a male visitor, he slaps and lambastes her for her castrating professionalism in her handling of clients and pours out all his resentment against the welfare system. After he leaves, Katherine cries for the first time in years and realizes "there was a lifetime of weeping before her but she did not know why" (p. 282). Oates understands, as Katherine does not, that she has let her professional self engulf her identity as a woman, that professional competence often extracts a high price in a woman's emotional health, that many men carry an inevitable resentment against any woman who has authority over them, and that many women are hopelessly dependent upon male approval to sanction their self-esteem.

Another professional woman who finds herself in a similar situation is Nora, the university professor of "Magna Mater." Nora is a highly respected scholar who is puritanically dedicated to the view that art grows not "out of ordinary, routine, emotional life" but "from a higher consciousness altogether" (p. 205) and who is most happy when immersed in her work: "When she spoke of her work she seemed to move into another dimension entirely—she was not the overweight, perspiring, rather too anxious hostess, but a consciousness entirely freed of the body, of all temporal limitations" (p. 204). But Nora's personal life intrudes upon her professional detachment. Plagued with disquieting relationships with all the males in her life, she yet needs male approval. Her husband has left her for a younger, more attractive woman, and her father, also a famous scholar, is ill and seems to have lost interest in Nora and her work. She finds her precocious, unstable son irrationally demanding and accusing and his male psychiatrist disrespectfully probing and insinuating. To complete the medley of unhappy relationships, one of her colleagues, Mason Colebrook, nastily tells her of a poem written about her by a former male student entitled "How Leda Got the Swan." Later, in a drunken release of inhibition, he pours out all his contempt for her as a scholar and woman. When his wife attempts to apologize for the scene, he yells: "Nora's the same ugly old selfish sadistic bitch she's always been, she won't give a damn, will you, Nora?" (p. 208). But Nora does care: "How rude, how insufferable! She felt almost betrayed, once again betrayed by a man she had somehow believed . . . had somehow believed might admire her" (p. 209).

Mason's cruel accusation that Nora is an "ugly old selfish sadistic bitch" has some measure of truth. Nora is guilty of being "ugly" and "old"—or at least plain and middle-aged—and women are still frequently valued or devalued as women on standards of youth and beauty. Indeed, Nora has been attempting to keep her feminine ego intact after her husband has deserted her for a twenty-four-year-old woman. Secondly, Nora has been "selfishly" dedicated to her work throughout her life. The "decade of research, teaching, and motherhood madly combined" angered her husband, "not liking the hurried meals, her distraction when he spoke of his work." He is also annoyed that *she* should make the "name *Drexler* known in the Cambridge–Boston–New York area, as if it were truly her name and not his" (p. 187). It is also implied that her father lost interest in her when his daughter's success and fame threatened to outstrip his own. Her son resents her selfish appropriation of a part of her time for her work and for friends, whereas he demands the rights of a son, her undivided attention. Finally, Nora is a "sadistic bitch." In the name of standards of academic excellence, she writes devastating reviews: "Nora shook her head helplessly, saying that she had hated to write that particular essay, knowing how it would hurt the author, she had truly *hated* to say such blunt, irrefutable things about the intelligence that had written it—but unfortunately 'someone had to do it,' she said" (p. 206). Obviously, she is deceiving herself. She does not hate to do such work, but positively relishes it. She takes a delight akin to the sadistic in destroying her opponent and in the process affirming her own superiority as a brilliant thinker, graceful writer of "loving cadences," and undaunted protectress of excellence. Nora's critical reviews are the sublimated expression of her resentment against men. Intellectually if not sexually she has the upper hand, and it wields the castrating knife.

Yet Nora cannot be so easily dismissed with a disparaging diagnosis. She exemplifies the dilemma of the professional woman in Oates's fictional world—if not, indeed, in life. The qualities which make for Nora's success as a scholar—her lucid intelligence, uncompromising standards, aggressive arguments and refutations, cool self-assurance, unstinting dedication to her work—all serve to undermine her image as a woman in the eyes of her family, friends, colleagues, and acquaintances. Others besides Mason Colebrook accuse Nora of sadistic dominion over men. Her former student sees her as Leda getting the Swan. Her son fantasizes that Nora murdered his father, and he has a recurrent dream where she deliberately drowns him. But Oates offers a balanced view of Nora. She is intellectually arrogant yet highly competent, sadistic in her reviews yet dedicated to her research and to the upholding of academic standards, self-deceived yet deceived by others, dependent upon the acceptance and praise of others yet capable of carrying on alone. A "magna mater" she is not, however, except in the most destructive sense of the term. Deeply ambivalent about the messy and distracting role of mother, she is excessively impatient with her son, demanding from him a maturity and rationality which this severely unstable child is incapable of. One of Dennis's recurrent nightmares is that a devouring mouth is in the room with him, a fantasy which—along with his compulsive eating—seems to express his regression to the oral phase of libidinal development, a frequent Oatesian pattern. Overcome with separation anxiety, Dennis's infantile response is to fantasize being devoured, drowned, or abandoned, and he attempts to overcome his fears in part through oral gratification, stuffing his overweight body with Ritz crackers. He is a whiny, obnoxious, cruel child largely because Nora's unconscious rejection and her guilty compensations for it create out of their relationship a sick little society of two, increasingly cut off from other human beings.

Nora has juggled her various roles as daughter, woman, mother, wife, scholar, and professor with uneven success. Despite her professional stature, she will never be a liberated woman. Emotionally insecure, she is too entangled in unsatisfactory relationships with men and too vulnerable to their demands and taunts, praise and criticism, attention and inattention.

With Jenny, Katherine, and Nora, Oates is showing that women's professional success compounds their problems in dealing with female sexuality. There is no such thing as neuter ground in Oates's stories, no professional equality for men and women. Women are different biologically, emotionally, psychically, and socially; and their sexuality necessarily enters into all facets of their lives, complicating their relationships with colleagues, clients, and students. The tensions and adjustments demanded by their professional selves, in turn, rebound on their personal relationships with lovers, husbands, and children. Women are intruders in the male world of professionalism. The violence and aggression which for men is often a healthy release of emotion effects for women—when channeled into the competitive drive for success—an unhealthy inhibiting and hardening of emotion. Competent women are often seen by the men with whom they work as usurpers of the male role and by the men with whom they deal professionally as castrators of male sexuality. But the most damaging repercussions of a woman's professionalism exist not in the way that others view her, but in the way she feels about herself as a woman. Sexuality is the ultimate reality for men and women in Oates's world, and women pay for their professional success with precious coin, stifled sexual identities. In so doing, they assure their perpetual nonliberation.

But the vast majority of Oates's women do not have careers. Their problem is not in reconciling a variety of selves but in coping with selflessness. They are not desexed by their aggressive intrusion into the male world but devitalized by their acquiescence to female vacuousness. Women are victims of an inadequate model of female selfhood. Those very qualities which are considered to be prototypically feminine—passivity, fragility, beauty, sensitivity, and dependence—make many women vulnerable to the harshness of modern life, insufficiently resilient to cope with life's unpredictability. The Oatesian woman's characteristic pose is sitting around waiting for something to happen or building an impenetrable wall around the self so that nothing can happen, or seeking, consciously or unconsciously, her own death. Oates's work offers a disturbing view of women's incapacity as a group to deal successfully with their sexuality and as a result with experience. It would be simplistic, however, to conclude that all that is necessary is an orgasmic release equivalent to Elena's in *Do With Me What You Will*. Most of Oates's women are so emotionally withdrawn that they are incapable of any degree of healthy sexuality. Oates does not offer any ready solutions. Of course, she has not encompassed the full range of women's possibilities in her fiction. Instead, focusing her attention upon certain recurrent types of unliberated women, she exposes the sexual roots of female nonliberation.

III   The Hungry Ghosts: *Academic Satire*

In *The Hungry Ghosts: Seven Allusive Comedies* she isolates another group of unliberated people—academics. To be read with pleasure and wincing by those familiar with the academic world, Joyce Carol Oates's satire probably has limited appeal to readers outside of academe. The title, as Oates explains on a front page, is an allusion to ancient Buddhist cosmology in which "A *preta* (ghost) . . haunts the earth's surface, continually driven by hunger—that is, desire of one kind or another."[6] The driving hungers of academics are channeled into guises painfully familiar to inhabitants of that world. As the subtitle makes clear, these stories are "comedies," written in a much lighter vein than is usual for Oates. She mockingly looks at the fears and phobias, the stock characters and situations of the so-called ivory-tower life: the insecurity, intimidation, and neuroses of graduate students; the personal vendettas and the sexual interests which influence hiring and firing; the cruelty, cowardice, plagiarism, pedantry, jealousy, and rivalry among academic peers; the pressures of publish or perish; the desire for fame and the dread of it. Characters pilloried include the popular black professor currying his Harvard-dandified whiteness; the provocatively dressed woman deploring sexism; the aging one-theory professor riding his hobbyhorse; the kindly, cowardly chairman avoiding decision-making; the predictably dressed poet plumping the departmental bibliography with publications in obscure magazines and newspapers.

The satiric intent limits the resonance of these stories, distinguishing them from Oates's best. Four take place at the same fictional university, Hilberry, located in southwestern Ontario, and feature some recurring characters.[7] These are "allusive" comedies because the titles of the stories are often taken from famous works such as John Bunyan's *Pilgrim's Progress,* Friedrich Nietzsche's *The Birth of Tragedy,* Alec de Tocqueville's *Democracy in America,* and William Blake's *Descriptive Catalogue.* But these borrowed titles take on new ironic meanings in these radically differing contexts. "Pilgrims' Progress," for example, depicts Saul Bird's messianic role as a charismatic, egotistical, flamboyant instructor who corrosively disrupts the staid academic world. He leads his "pilgrims," Wanda and Erasmus, out of their lonely, insecure, and conventional lives as college instructors into a life of "relevant" teaching, clique identification, and campus demonstrations, only to desert them and to skip town when they have thoroughly damaged their careers. Barry, the graduate assistant of Dr. Thayer in "The Birth of Tragedy," discovers not only that the essence of tragedy is "freedom" when he departs from his frantically prepared lecture and talks in impromptu fashion to Thayer's class, but he simultaneously acts out his own tragedy and asserts his own freedom from Thayer's hobbyhorse scholarship, homosexual advances, arrogance, and paternalism, indeed, probably from the world of academics altogether, since Thayer has taperecorded the session and is self-protective and vindictive enough to use it to eject Barry from Hilberry.

Two of the most successful stories of the collection are "Democracy in America" and "A Descriptive Catalogue." In the first not only is Tocqueville one of the subjects of Ronald Pauli's manuscript, but the story is a particularly vivid account of the tortures and hazards of securing an identity in America where the extent of one's upward mobility and professional status is "democratically" determined by the success of one's efforts and where those efforts may be unfairly jeopardized by the carelessness of others. The story records Ronald's traumatic but ultimately successful attempt to retrieve the pages of his manuscript from the room of the slovenly free-lance copyeditor who had died before completing his work. Here Oates depicts with nightmarish elaboration the worst fear of all writers, the irretrievable loss of the manuscript. Ronald is forced in his desperation to defy the stench, filth, and total disarray of Dietrich's room—even his bathroom—to retrieve one by one the precious battered and torn pages of his book. He comes to see this book as more than just a sheaf of pages, but the tattered pieces of his own identity. For Oates is incisive in recognizing just how much of an academic's identity is sometimes invested in the belabored prose of these scholarly efforts. Ronald's horrendous experience in Dietrich's room becomes a personal crisis. Without his book Ronald is not sure that he exists; with it he secures his tenuous hold on himself: "His manuscript was crumpled, torn, stained with the dirt of a total stranger, but it had not been destroyed. And he had not been destroyed. 'I'm still living,' Ronald whispered" (p. 29). This theme of publish-or-perish is played out in equally effective form in "A Descriptive Catalogue."

The title refers specifically to Reynold Mason's published article on "Blake's concept of heroic painting, as set forth in his *Descriptive Catalogue*" (p. 82); but, more germane to the irony of the story, it also applies to his rival Ron Blass's numerous contributions to the department's bibliography. Oates's comedy is unrestrained as she describes his fully documented entries: poems with long titles written out and amply spaced, reviews in the local newspaper, readings at the local pub, talks on the university television station, and an exact count—358 poems in 53 little-known magazines with titles like *Sink* and *Rejects*. The conflict arises when Mason accuses Blass of plagiarism and a special committee is formed to investigate the charges. Mason convincingly demonstrates Ron's borrowings from a 1941 poem by Samuel Gregory. Ron's version adds Cummingslike typography and pop-culture diction:

> i'm going
>> where climates don't fail
>> fields fly-filled OK
>> curdled lilies OK
> i'm going
>>> into the tides
>>> into the smell
>> of
>> the
> sea. (p. 89–90)

But the crowning ironic twist is that another professor, Dr. May, observes that an earlier version of the poem called "Heaven-Haven" is by Hopkins. In this exposé of at least two generations of academic dishonesty Oates is deploring reprehensible behavior, to be sure, but she also mocks the academic environment which fosters the quantitative measure of scholarly production. Ron's "borrowings" were brought on by the ever-present pressure to publish or perish. Wanting to be well liked and to please the chairman, having to support a wife and family, and being convinced that "it could be anything . . . nobody seems to read it" (p. 94), Ron turns to plagiarism when he felt he must publish even though he had nothing to say. In the final ironic twist of this excellent story, the satiric target is less on Ron's shoddy poetry than on his colleagues' cowardice, for Ron's surreptitious distribution of information about the legal definitions of plagiarism and the possibility for a resultant slander suit secures a vote in favor of his retention.

Obviously, the academic world is not as bad as Oates paints it in this volume, but the kernel of truth in these exaggerated tales demonstrates her familiarity with the milieu and contributes to the witty, comic, and at times biting satire. Other allusive stories—reimaginings of literary masterpieces—are not conceived as "comedies" but as "spiritual marriages" between Oates and her famous precursors.

IV   Marriages and Infidelities: *Short Story Masterpieces Revisited*

Joyce Carol Oates insists that she is writing within a "strong tradition" of other writers; the most interesting acknowledgment of her debt to other writers is her "reimagining" of famous stories, several of which are collected in *Marriages and Infidelities*. Her "spiritual marriages," as she describes them,[8] to these famous writers are part of the volume's thematic unity as "a book of marriages. Some are conventional marriages of men and women, others are marriages in another sense—with a phase of art, with something that transcends the limitations of the ego."[9] Some stories, such as "The Lady with the Pet Dog" and "The Metamorphosis," closely parallel the originals, while others, such as "Where I Lived, and What I Lived For," bear no thematic or formal resemblance to the originals and could only have been envisioned as startling ironic contrasts. Some, like "The Dead," fall somewhere in between these two extremes—stories unique and effective in their own right, which are further enriched by borrowings from and allusions to famous works by other authors.

Oates's "The Lady with the Pet Dog" closely resembles Anton Chekhov's similarly titled story. In terms of context and theme this story is similar to many of Oates's others. It focuses on an adulterous affair initiated at a beach resort, supposedly terminated at the end of the couple's holidays, and resumed clandestinely after an encounter at a concert. Chekhov's Yalta becomes Nantucket Island; nineteenth-century Russia becomes twentieth-century America; the man's perspective shifts to that of the woman; and many of the details such as the ownership of the pet dog that conveniently precipitates conversation between the two and the order of telling of the events are changed. Oates embellishes the lives of the characters and the details of the story. The husband now has a blind son with him on vacation; he casually sketches Anna when they first meet on the beach. But the two stories are nearly identical in theme and basic outline. Both record the guilt of Anna over the affair, the unsuccessful attempts to resume separate married lives, the emotional meeting in the concert hall, and the climactic, joyful moment of revelation later in a hotel room—preceded in both versions by the man's sight of himself in a mirror—that this allegedly sinful affair must go on, that it embodies a truth to feeling, a love, that their staid, conventional marriages lack.

Oates's story is less imagined than transposed, less an original creation than an exercise. Her story is effective, but in the same way that Chekhov's is. Her reinterpretation of Franz Kafka's "The Metamorphosis," while still closely paralleling the original, diverges in significant ways from it. Here, however, the result is a story which is undeniably inferior to Kafka's masterpiece.

Oates has attempted to transform the phantasmagoric into the realistically credible, but not without sacrificing the heart of Kafka's macabre fable, the horror and fascination generated by Gregor Samsa's metamorphosis into a gigantic insect. In Oates's "The Metamorphosis" exactly what happens to Matthew Brown is not specified. While at work, he feels himself to be the recipient of someone else's dream (the story was originally entitled "Others' Dreams"[10]) in which he sees himself as a mummy wrapped in blankets in bed. He drives himself home, feels his legs to be weakening and his body to be emitting a foul odor, and locks himself in his bedroom. It is credible that a man could all of sudden be stricken with an odious illness. In this realistic context the theme is the same as in Kafka's version: the precariousness of a person's being, the inexplicable threat that can strike one unaware. Moreover, Oates again gives her story a contemporary, particularized setting. Kafka's traveling salesman becomes Matthew Brown, a successful, well-dressed, well-preserved, forty-six-year-old American salesman who has been selling new cars for twenty years at Overmeyer Ford. He knows how to handle customers and his mind is filled, even in his illness, with the jargon of his trade.

But what is gained in Oates's story in particularity and realism is lost in the fascinatingly macabre details of Gregor's attempts to cope with his unwieldy insect's body. In spite of his condition, he is pathetically bent on doing his duty; in spite of the ingratitude and selfishness which surface in his employer and family, he bears no malice. In contrast, Matthew is only semiconscious of his condition, his duty, and his responsibility to those around him. Oates employs italicized sections showing the responses of his children and wife; their bewildered, embarrassed, sometimes angry reactions to the illness do not carry with them the indictment often implicit in Kafka's incisive portraits of Gregor's father, mother, and sister. For although Oates adds more characters to her version, they are not vividly realized as separate individuals. The realistic details diffuse and obscure rather than enhance the original thematic statement and characterization. Kafka's story is powerful precisely because it boldly employs the phantasmagoric, which Oates fails to attempt here, although she occasionally does, as in her startling reimagining of a chapter from Henry David Thoreau's *Walden*.

Her "Where I Lived, and What I Lived For" is a strange tale which takes the form of alternating monologues of a bloodthirsty pursuer and his prey, a tired and terrified man. One assumes that the pursuer is a figment of the prey's imagination. He admits to making up other fictions to dramatize his life. The cannibalistic, tireless pursuer who obliterates the man's footsteps with his size-thirteen shoes is probably one of his fictions, part of his attempt to give shape to his terror and to his conception of life as an endless chase. What does this have to do with Thoreau? This man is Thoreau's antithesis, a man who does not view time as the "stream" to "go a-fishing in," but as a perpetual chase during which it is "in the nature of the pursued to outwit the millions of people pursuing him, all those people who want to take his place, his possessions, the food he has left uneaten, his wrist watch, his very skin" (p. 322).[11] Oates's character is a man who does not "live deliberately," who does not seek "simplicity, simplicity, simplicity," and who does not "crave only reality" (as Thoreau does), but who only fabricates self-deluding fictions; a man who does not find joy in sucking "all the marrow of life," but who fears a sadistic pursuer who wants to suck the blood out of his life!: "Eating on the run is no good—I'm still hungry—I could seize him and sink my teeth into his throat, why not? Suck his blood so that it runs down my chin, my chest; why not?" (p. 322).

Oates's grotesque tale of the prey's fear of the pursuer's gleeful, bloodthirsty cannibalism is an effective way of dramatizing through phantasmagoria the terrifying, feverish chase that is contemporary life for modern man. To contrast this self-victimized man with nineteenth-century Thoreau highlights a shocking loss of independence, optimism, and joy. The parallel enhances Oates's own highly original story; it serves to broaden its thematic implications.

Her reworking of James Joyce's "The Dead" is also successful. Although the story parallels Joyce's in structure and theme and even duplicates its language and symbolism at times, the situation is quite different. The central character of Oates's story, Ilena Williams, is a college teacher and novelist whose recent popular novel has turned her, somewhat uncomfortably, into a minor celebrity. Gabriel Conroy, her counterpart in Joyce's story, is a newspaper reviewer rather than artist but he, too, as master of ceremonies at his aunts' Christmas party, is temporarily in the public limelight.[12] Both stories focus on the emotional sterility of the central character, which is matched by the stultifying "dead" environments in which they live.

Oates is devastating in her depiction of the staid academic environment of the small Catholic university in Detroit where Ilena is employed before she is dismissed for refusing to pass the master's oral exam of a student, a Brother, who could not define "Gothicism" or the "heroic couplet," could not discuss a Shakespearean sonnet or define the sonnet or give any examples of a sonnet, could not talk about any poem at all or name his favorite poem or name the title of any poem. (The other members of the committee, amusingly and predictably, want to give him a "B"!) Like Joyce's story, Oates's reverberates with references to dead people and things. Ilena's book is entitled *Death Dance*. At parties the assassination of President Kennedy, the waste of Vietnam, the death of the NAACP are mentioned. In the worst moments of Ilena's marriage, her husband urges her to die. She recognizes that the endless pills she takes to cope with life are a kind of "substitute death." As a teacher she preaches the right to birth control and death control, a right which she at times considers exercising. At the end of the story, she learns of the death of her former student, Emmett Norlan.

Ilena, who becomes involved in one sexual liaison after another, feels a progressive deadening of response: "with Lyle her body was dead, worn out, it could not respond to his most tender caresses. She felt how intellectualized she had become, her entire body passive and observant and cynical" (pp. 396–97). Gabriel, in contrast, awakened sexually by the sight of his wife in a pensive mood at the party, desires to "forget the years of dull existence together and to remember only their moments of ecstasy." Gabriel's final epiphanic self-revelation is thus more shocking to him than Ilena's, because he has been until then totally unaware of his emotional sterility, yet Oates's story closely follows Joyce's in the final few pages. Where ill-fated Michael Furey and his pure love for Gretta cause Gabriel to realize that he has been incapable of love, news of the death of Ilena's former student, Emmett Norlan, similarly awakens in her a realization that she has been incapable of responding to the potential communion once offered to her by this student or by anyone else. Recognizing that she has had too many lovers, too much physical contact and too little spiritual communion, she feels that she is fading away, dissolving into death: "Ilena was conscious of something fading in her, in the pit of her belly. Fading. Dying. *The central sexual organ is the brain,* she had read, and now her brain was drawing away, fading, dissolving" (p. 409). The language echoes Joyce's famous description of Gabriel's movement toward death: "His own identity was fading out into a gray impalpable world: the solid world itself, which these dead had one time reared and lived in, was dissolving and dwindling." Similarly, the snow, emblematic of death, lies on Ilena's lover's coat as it does on Gabriel's. As it falls "upon all the living and the dead" in the magnificent ending of Joyce's story, so also does it in Oates's, and Ilena like Gabriel swoons toward death: "Her brain seemed to swoon backward into an elation of fatigue, and she heard beyond this man's hoarse, strained breathing the gentle breathing of the snow, falling shapelessly upon them all" (p. 409).

Of course, Oates's story does not achieve here or elsewhere the sheer eloquence of Joyce's. By using such closely parallel passages, she risks the discrediting of her own achievement, but I think the gamble is successful. Autonomous and well-realized in its own right, the story achieves through its literary parallel a breadth of generalization impossible without it. Ilena shares a sterility not only with the other inhabitants of her world, but also with the lost souls of Joyce's *Dubliners,* and indeed of the world. Oates invites the reader to reexperience the Joycean story, while she offers a contemporary re-creation of it.

Oates's reimaginings of famous short stories take several forms, some more successful than others.[13] It is to her credit that she dares to invite comparison with the most exceptional masters of the short story and even more to her credit that this literary inspiration has so often led her to fashion unique and memorable stories. That she honors these literary precursors in her reworking of their stories is also apparent, since the effort includes a humble recognition that she is writing within a strong tradition which will unconsciously if not consciously shape her own writing. Her humility extends so far in another short-story collection, *The Poisoned Kiss,* that she disclaims authorship altogether!

V The Poisoned Kiss: *Alien Authorship*

Oates attributes *The Poisoned Kiss* to an imaginary author, "Ferandes de Briao." She claims to be merely the translator of tales from an imaginary Portuguese work, *Azulejos.* Attempting to explain this curious phenomenon both in a prefatory note and a two-and-one-half-page afterword to the volume, she claims to be as mystified by the inspiration of these stories as the reader is likely to be by her disclaimers of authorship. She explains that she first experienced this alien authorship in November 1970 while she was preoccupied with her "own" writing: "If I did not concentrate deliberately on my own work, or if I allowed myself to daydream or become overly exhausted, my mind would move—it would seem to swerve or leap—into 'Portugal.' There seemed to be a great pressure, a series of visions, that demanded a formal, aesthetic form; I was besieged by Ferandes—story after story, some no more than sketches or paragraphs that tended to crowd out my own writing" (pp. 187–89).[14] Although she claims to "prefer the synthesis of the 'existential' and the 'timeless' of my own fiction" and would like to comprehend and to explain rationally the creation of these stories as merely "metaphorical," she cannot: "But in truth none of it was metaphorical, any more than you and I are metaphorical." An exceptional ability to imagine and to create characters and experiences seemingly antithetical to herself has always been typical of Oates's method. Here she carries the process further; it is not just her characters but "herself" who is imagined as a dandified, middle-aged Portuguese man of culture and letters. Thematically these stories are not alien to Oates's canon.

Just as this volume apparently grew out of a mysterious, uninvited bond to an alien self, the stories explore in a variety of contexts the mysterious and uninvited bonds of various characters to people, places, behavior, and aspects of themselves alien and antithetical to their conscious personalities. Like Oates, her characters often cannot rationally explain or accept their compulsive bondage. The title of the volume effectively capsulizes its theme. It is about the "kiss"—an intimate bond between the self and an "other"—but a kiss which is "poisoned" because this union is so disquieting and inexplicable; it brings the individual so little joy. The title story, a page-and-a-half sketch, presents the theme as bald parable. The first-person narrator, in his determined effort to unite himself with his loved one, whose kiss haunts his dreams, obliterates the obstacles standing in his way. He pushes one stranger, chokes another, and shoves another into an open tomb. He is angered by their insensitivity to his special destiny, his all-consuming passion, his dangerous and determined quest. Although the brevity and lack of specificity of this sketch (duplicated in a number of other similar vignettes in the volume) are indeed atypical of Oates's other stories, the central matter—a character in the grips of a powerful passion—is at the heart of her fiction. Most of the other stories are similarly portrayals of characters driven by compulsions beyond their intellectual control.

Those which are closest to Oates's other fiction—a group encompassing most of the stories—depict characters whose compulsive behavior is psychologically explainable. Another small group of stories straddles the fence between the "real" and the "spiritual." One could explain the happenings in psychological terms, but since a spiritual realm is posited, a nonrational explanation is also possible. Finally, a few of the stories, the most unusual and atypical, are in the realm of fantasy—illustrative tall tales depicting unrealistic characters and actions.

The first group of stories portrays the compulsive attraction of alien lives, selves, people, or experiences, an attraction which is often "poisonous" because it disrupts the life of the protagonist. A number of these stories show a character's need for a stranger or strangers to confirm his individual selfhood. For example, the young bride in "Loss" finds a man watching her regularly as she lounges on the balcony of her apartment building. He responds sensitively to her, creating graceful prose translations of her appearance and movement:

"*a woman with a supple, full body, her skin gleaming, a woman absolutely at ease because she wants nothing*" (p. 31). The woman is pleased but disquieted by this attention. She deliberately provokes an angry scene with her husband on the balcony, an act which serves to stop forever the peeping Tomism of her neighbor. His disappearance shatters her self-esteem. Without this flattering reflection and imaginative re-creation she feels lost in her own anonymity: "There was no illumination, no picture of herself. She felt her body grow weak, as if emptying out. She wept because she was going to nothing, becoming nothing" (p. 37).

Some characters like the young man in "Sunlight/Twilight" gain identity through a bond to a victimizer. Brutally castrated, he is the recipient of his mother's pity and concern; but he dreams recurrently of his victimizer, to whom he feels bound in love as he does not to his mother. He is like the women in other Oates stories who gain some relief from an anonymous self through their brutalization by an assailant. Sometimes a character finds himself bound to a person whom he intellectually despises, who he feels is unworthy of his obsession, and who exposes a side of his nature that is difficult to accept. Such is Ferandes's obsession in "The Letter" with an illiterate, coarse, and slovenly young man to whom he has written a self-incriminating letter. He seeks to retrieve the letter and so to negate this "other" self and its compulsive need to communicate with this brutish young man.

The dictates of another self—an alien personality within the conscious self—are sometimes very strong indeed, as the man in "Distance" discovers. The story centers on the London sojourn of a meticulous, orderly, ambitious young Portuguese who works in his country's embassy. Having always lived a busy, complicated, ego-centered life, he is disgusted by the vagrants who reside in the park outside his dwelling. As he finds the anonymity of his life in a foreign country increasingly comfortable, his obsession with the vagrants intensifies. Consciously disapproving of their life-style, he is unconsciously drawn to their anonymity. By the end of the story, his obsession gets the best of him. He buys a bottle of dinner wine, puts it into a paper bag, and gradually approaches the men on the bench. The anonymous self of a vagrant—so alien to his conscious personality—takes over.

Some characters do not fight but welcome their metamorphoses into other selves, but they may be blocked from achieving them. Such is the plight of the "you" of "The Secret Mirror," a man who wishes to be a woman. This transvestite dresses himself lovingly in front of a secret mirror in a bridal outfit, a wig with copper-colored curls, and carefully applied theatrical makeup. He imagines his emergence into the street and the angry, derisive unmasking his appearance would provoke. So, instead of going out, he stares at himself in his secret mirror and weeps as he removes the disguise: "You are . . . weeping for your lost selves, whom no one can return to you, but who have slipped out of the mirror now, untouched, unpursued" (p. 91).

Sometimes the unacknowledged, anonymous self within is capable of criminal and insane behavior. The "you" of "In a Public Place" exploits his own anonymity and that of the "public place" by gratuitously murdering an old man who sits on a bench. The boy of "Patricide" has murdered his father but has so suppressed the murderous self that he can only recollect disconnected, nonincriminating facts before and after the incident: a "stranger" gives him an ax; it accidentally falls from his hands and cuts his foot; his father lies bleeding on the ground.

All of the aforementioned stories are essentially realistic, even though often particulars are left vague. In some stories, however, a spiritual realm coexistent with empirical reality is at least a possibility. For example, Dr. Thomaz in "The Cruel Master" posits a Master who requires him repeatedly to reexperience a dream in which he helplessly observes a young boy being trampled to death by a horse. By the end of the story his repulsion has turned to intense enjoyment. This "cruel master" could merely be the sadistic side of his being which he has always suppressed, or it could be an inhuman spiritual being.

By far the most interesting of this group of stories is "Plagiarized Material," a portrayal of Cabral, a poet and man of letters who gradually realizes that his literary selfhood is being taken over by other younger, more talented writers. He begins by discovering that an appreciative American critic has used language that directly echoes one of Cabral's own unfinished, unpublished stories, in fact employing his exact phrases and words. A short time later, after he works on some poetry, he runs across a poem by a young Polish poet which duplicates exactly the idea of his poem. The grim discoveries continue, all the more galling because his plagiarists "were much younger than he. They would outlive him. They bred shamelessly and multiplied, like the lowest forms of animal life" (p. 179). Finally he wills his own death in protest over the shameful appropriation of his unique selfhood, "cursing all the Plagiarists who sucked his life from him" (p. 181). Obviously, this "plagiarism" of his ideas, thoughts, and words cannot be explained away in rational and realistic terms. The story is either an explicit demonstration of the fluidity of the realm of "spirit," which makes possible the literal invasion and robbery of one's consciousness by other human beings, or it is a witty fantasy, a parable designed to demonstrate that writers indeed draw from the same vast communal consciousness and should be appropriately humbled by the fact, not infatuated with their own egos as is Cabral.

Two other stories in this volume are out-and-out fantasy parables, one depicting a wooden statue of the Virgin Mary with the infant Jesus who suffers a frozen empathy with her worshipers and the other depicting a son of God who rebels against his temperamental and tyrannical Father. "Our Lady of the Easy Death of Alferce" is told in the first person by the statue, who feels the intense love that is poured out by her worshipers. Her empathy is so great for the love and sorrow of one boy who fiercely stares at her that a tear forces itself out of her eye. She would like to hide it, but she is "fixed like stone." The boy is startled and then crazed by this miracle—*"For me? For me . . .?"* It precipitates even greater, almost unbearable, adoration of the statue who cannot move from her frozen posture: *"Don't love me, don't love . . .* my lips want to open in a shriek, *Don't love me"* (p. 22). One day the boy's mother pushes through the crowd, shouting at the statue: *"You are not Mary! You are a thief, a murderer!* she screams. *My son was poisoned by you—they have taken him away"* (p. 23). She attacks the statue, breaking off and carrying away the Child. Although workmen repair it and replace the Child with a wooden doll, the statue suffers in empathy with the sorrowful and tormented motherhood of this woman. Here too is a "poisoned kiss," a tenacious bond of love, which brings only grief and sorrow to the beings it unites.

Similarly, in "The Son of God and His Sorrow" a son of God finds his godliness brings only grief and sorrow to the people he helplessly loves. One day while blessing a village and promising a fine crop, he is overcome with the wretchedness of the villagers and breaks down and weeps. This so angers God that he brings a vicious storm which destroys the crop. The son can do nothing to help the people, since his well-intentioned love stirs the vengeful wrath of his temperamental Father:

I ran from them and my running caused wind to be sucked after me—whirlpools of air struck out at the countryside and devastated it up and down the coast for hundreds of miles.

Where I wept, where I passed, there were floods and tornadoes. . . .

For many days I lay in the dark. I prayed to God to forgive me, to allow me release and death, and in His spite He sent more torments upon me, for if I turned my head too sharply to one side—startled by a rat, perhaps—sudden storms would rush out in that direction, a hundred miles out into the countryside; if I turned my head too sharply to the other side, identical storms would rush out to sea. (p. 129)

Finally, overcome by the grief he is bringing to the world, he gets his mother to help nail him to a cross, and at the end of the story he awaits his own death. The perfect final touch is the hysterical shrieking of God: *"Always this happens! Always my sons disobey me!"* (p. 131).

"The Son of God and His Sorrow," and other stories from *The Poisoned Kiss* such as "Distance" and "Plagiarized Material," stand with the finest of Oates's fiction. While the volume is an interesting technical departure from the existential realism of most of her fiction, she has often used the short story as the experimental laboratory for her fiction. Here she performs an experiment which is largely successful, however much she may disclaim authorship.

CHAPTER 7

The Achievement: Rhetoric and Reader

NURTURED by modern psychology and philosophy, Joyce Carol Oates's characterization is modernist in conception, but her dominant method has been traditional, almost anachronistic in form. A seemingly clinical report of the debilitating effects of familial and environmental limitations, much of her fiction falls within the tradition of American Naturalism, but its visionary perspective counters the determinism usually associated with Naturalism. These anomalies raise problems in interpretation, and sometimes prevent Oates's work from communicating effectively with an audience. As I stated at the outset of this study, I do not think that Joyce Carol Oates's work very often finds the participatory readership she desires; by that I mean that the "complex propositions about the nature of personality" which she puts forward through her fiction are not given serious consideration by many readers. Rather oddly, her fiction appears to appeal at an emotional level to one audience while being directed rhetorically to another. Using the term "rhetoric of fiction" in its broader sense, as Wayne C. Booth does in his book of that title, to mean the total effect of all the components of a work rather than in its narrower sense to refer to the overt, distinguishable voice of the author, I have to conclude, finally, that the rhetorical effect of Oates's work is sometimes impaired or blurred by an incomplete fusion of the components of her art. I suggest this after attempting to assess my own responses to her fiction along with those of my students, colleagues, and friends, and of reviewers and critics. The responses of a number of discerning readers point often to an apparent disharmony of subject and form and of emotional impact and thematic statement at the heart of some of Oates's works.

Most readers place Oates within the tradition of American Naturalism, an identification that is understandable in terms of her subject matter and method, but one which contributes to a misunderstanding of her visionary perspective. Oates's early work in particular, detailing the sordid, brutal, dehumanized lives of inarticulate people, seems to be the very essence of Naturalism. Three early novels form a trilogy of American social groups, each depicting characters both psychologically maimed by constricting, unnurturing familial bonds and economically and spiritually oppressed by a discriminatory social system based on competitive, materialistic values. *A Garden of Earthly Delights,* in its depiction of descendants of migrant workers, is perhaps evocative of John Steinbeck's *The Grapes of Wrath. them,* in its portrayal of the crushing urban environment of the poor, is perhaps reminiscent of Theodore Dreiser's works and of Harriette Arnow's *The Dollmaker,* which Oates admires.[1] All in all, the dominant impression Oates's work makes on both casual readers and literary scholars is of the devastating intensity and ubiquity of violence and of the seemingly unrelieved impotence and powerlessness of her characters in a "tragically diminished urban world."[2] Furthermore, Oates's fictional craftsmanship contributes to her identification as a naturalistic writer.

In this time of radical experimentation with novelistic form, she has been drawn until recently to basically a linear narrative, reported by a reliable, omniscient narrator who retains a Zolalike clinical detachment. While many of her short stories do have experimental structures, her novels before *The Assassins* do not. To be sure, she often uses counterpoint, and her novels contain some structural innovations like the letter to "Joyce Carol Oates" which interrupts the narrative in *them,* or the legal-brief format of *Do With Me What You Will,* but straightforward, third-person narrative is the dominant mode of six of her first seven novels (*Expensive People* employs first-person point of view). She implies that her concern with imbuing her novels with social significance makes the more restricted, personal scope of novelists like Woolf and Beckett inappropriate: "Since I am a novelist in the tradition, let us say, of Dickens and Dostoyevsky and Stendhal rather than of Virginia Woolf and Samuel Beckett, I am always concerned with the larger social/political/moral implications of my characters' experiences. In other words, I could not take the time to write about a group of people who did not represent, in their various struggles, fantasies, unusual experiences, hopes, etc., our society in miniature."[3] Yet she also describes herself as a "psychological realist"[4] and, indeed, in her focus on the internal lives of her characters—their obsessions, neuroses, confusions, and madnesses—she is distinctly modernist in spirit. An odd coupling of a modernist conception of character with traditionalist form is a basic feature of her art. As John Ditsky has observed: "Superficially similar to realistic fiction, yet tonally aligned with the experimentalists, her fiction shares the latter group's concern with inner states—no longer quite the same as a character's 'psychology,' but the fragmented reflection by his mind of the fragmented external world."[5] Because she draws parallels between "inner states" and "the fragmented external world," because, that is, she develops the social as well as the psychological context, details objective reality as well as subjective experience, she clings to the realistic mode. Sometimes she undertakes ambitious parallels between the lives of her characters and the state of our culture. In *Wonderland,* for example, living in the human body parallels living in society; cancer is biological and sociological; personal problems reflect social movements; the loss of a father duplicates the loss of a president.

Oates's intent, however, is not merely to detail what T. S. Eliot calls "the immense panorama of futility and anarchy which is contemporary history,"[6] but rather to suggest that transcendence of this world is possible, that the fragments are part of a single totality. If it is true as Charles Child Walcutt has suggested in *American Literary Naturalism* (1956) that works in this mode have become a "divided stream" which has at its source the monistic vision of the Transcendentalists, then Joyce Carol Oates is attempting to make that stream flow again as one.

Central to Oates's thought and to her work is a visionary conception of human experience, a belief that the ego-consciousness of our culture can be transcended personally and collectively, a vision of the profane world as simultaneously "paradise," of the physical and the spiritual worlds as "not two at all, but one,"[7] of man not isolated by personal and historical roles but united in the single family of man. Oates claims that this visionary perspective informs *them* and her other fiction:

In *them* I deal in utter seriousness with the possibility of the transformation of our culture by eastern religion—at least the "mysticism" of the Indian saint who teaches, contrary to what America teaches Maureen and Jules, that "we are all members of a single family." If people are miserable today it must be that they identify far too deeply with their historical roles. So in my fiction I try to show that the local, the private, the family-determined, the political, the accidental, is to be transcended through an identification with the ahistorical. (Many American writers do this, I believe—the transcendence is usually through a union or interest in nature, sometimes through political activity, sometimes a directly "religious" identification. . . . Since I interpret most activities that take the individual out of his claustrophobic ego-role as "religious," I suppose I am in some vague way a "religious" writer, though not in any conventional sense. And I want not at all to be called a "religious writer"!) I really do believe that, in ways quite beyond my own understanding, there will be a gradual transformation of consciousness in the West, and that, as is perhaps often the case with neurotics the "problem" will never be solved but simply outgrown and forgotten. And new problems will arise— since it is our privilege to live melodramatically.[8]

But apparently this informing vision is sometimes not sufficiently integrated into the form and design of her works. While the writer cannot be blamed for inattentive reading, too often readers nonetheless have missed the groping toward wholeness within the devastatingly fragmented lives of her characters. That readers have, for example, persistently missed the "spiritual rebirth" of Jules Wendall in the Detroit riot in *them* suggests that this event, critical to interpretation of the novel, is not given the emphasis it needs. A number of contributing causes may make this so.

First, it may be that Oates's vision—lacking support from commonly shared myths and ideologies in our culture—is too private and alien to be acceptable to her readers. Unable to accept, for example, the idea of liberation through violence, some readers see Jules's murder of the policeman simply as a gratuitous act. Indeed, *them* is a very troublesome book to assess because of the difficulty of knowing exactly how far the parody of the naturalistic mode and resultant irony extend. In one sense Jules is not to blame for the murder because he has been set in opposition to authoritarian structures all his life by his very poverty and ghetto-rearing. A policeman early in the novel identified himself as Jules's enemy; Jules is responding in kind. His environment has programmed him for this response which is preferable to cowed submission, just as the riot is preferable to hopeless apathy. If so, then this liberating violence is an ironic reversal of the usual outcome of a naturalistic novel: where the protagonist is usually thwarted by his environment, here Jules is ironically freed; he's on his way to California to "some sort of American success." He is both a hero and a murderer at once which Oates says "I think . . . is ironic. I hope it is."[9] Yet Jules at the end of the novel seems to be returned to the bouyant, ebullient self he was before his "spiritual death," and although he may be naive about his ability to shape a successful future, he unlike his sister is open to the possibilities of experience. In this sense he is genuinely, not ironically, a "hero." Not surprisingly, many readers cannot or will not accept him as both a murderer and as a likeable, joyful young man.

In addition to interpreting satisfactorily, or accepting, "violent liberation," readers also have difficulty knowing how to view Oates's portrayal of compulsive sexual attraction. Few other fiction writers have dwelt with such obsession upon the "pain and risk" of love, the torture and unhappiness that are sometimes concomitant with sexual relationships. Yet Oates claims that her "characters generally fall in love with people who will unlock a 'higher' self in them."[10] Often sexual union seems to be a way to open up a constricted self. Shar and Karen (*With Shuddering Fall*), Lowry and Clara (*A Garden*), Jules and Nadine (*them*), Jesse and Reva (*Wonderland*), Elena and Jack (*Do With Me*) are locked in compulsive and tortuous relationships, yet some of the language describing these relationships suggests liberation to a "higher self" through sexual union is possible. For example, Jules with Nadine feels "a great joy began in him; he wanted to gather her violently into his arms and penetrate her to the very kernel of her being, to her deepest silence, bringing her to a release of this joy" (p. 381); he feels "translated beyond himself, transfigured" (p. 383). Jesse contemplating a union with Reva feels "as if the hot, hollow, radiant core of his being, the elusive Jesse itself, were very close to his grasp" (p. 355). While these unions do not liberate because of a holding back of one or both of the partners, Elena Howe does indeed awaken to fuller selfhood through orgasmic love with Jack in *Do With Me What You Will*. One must conclude, I think, that Oates shares in some ways D. H. Lawrence's belief in the possibility of a "baptism of fire in passion." But Lawrence, unlike Oates, explains at length within the context of his fiction the significance he attributes to sexuality and thus makes public the components of his private vision. While one may balk at Lawrence's "preachiness," yet without either more explicit rhetoric or more success in these unions, the reader may not see these largely agonizing relationships as a means potentially towards liberating selfhood, for there is so little spontaneous joy in Oates's work. Moreover, so many of her characters, viscerally uncomfortable with their bodies, are quite incapable of any sort of Lawrentian "blood-consciousness." Oates senses that D. H. Lawrence was deeply ambivalent about erotic love:

One feels that he writes to discover what he thinks, what is thinking in him, on an unconscious level. Love is an ecstatic experience. Or is it, perhaps, a delusion? Erotic love is a way of salvation—or is it a distraction, a burden? Is it something to be gone through in order that one's deepest self may be stirred to life? Or is it a very simple, utterly natural emotion? . . . Lawrence does not really know, regardless of his dogmatic remarks about "mind-consciousness" and "blood-consciousness." He cannot *know;* he must continually strive to know, and accept continual frustration.[11]

So too does one sense that Joyce Carol Oates does not truly *know* whether sexual love is an ecstatic experience or a delusion, a transcending experience or "a delirium and a pathological condition" making "of the lover a crazed man; his blood leaps with bacteria that shoots the temperature up toward death" (*them,* p. 274). Her ambivalence is recorded in her texts causing the confused responses of her readers who in turn don't know how much irony is implicit in the language describing these unions. Perhaps it is being simplistic to insist that writers sort out their ambivalence when all they can do is "strive to know," work through their own inchoate experiences of writing and, as Virginia Woolf put it, "record the atoms as they fall," but nonetheless paradoxical irresolution, however modern a condition, is deeply unsettling to many readers, especially if it is found in a novel which appears in other ways to be conventional and straightforward.

Similarly, many readers find Oates's work excessively depressing because her characters seem so troubled, neurotic, violent, restless, or anti-social. Yet Oates claims such individuals are ripe for liberation, straining to grow. She claims to have a "heretical or unusual theory of the 'neuroses' ":

I don't believe in them at all, but see them (in my friends and students, as well as in my fictional characters) as symptoms of restlessness, a normal and desirable straining against the too-close confines of a personality now outgrown, or a social "role" too restrictive. Therefore, in my fiction, the troubled people are precisely those who yearn for a higher life—those in whom the life-form itself is stirring. By singling out individuals who are representative of our society and who, as people, interest me very much, I attempt to submerge myself in that foreign personality and see *how* and *why* and *to what end* the behaviour that people call "anti-social" or "neurotic" is actually functioning. And it is always my discovery that these people are genuinely superior to the role in life, the social station, the economic level, the marriage, the job, the philosophical beliefs, etc., in which they find themselves. They must have liberation, room to grow in. . . . So, it is the restless who interest me, as a novelist, for only out of restlessness can higher personalities emerge, just as, in a social context, it is only out of occasional surprises and upheavals that new ways of life can emerge.[12]

Again, without more guidance the reader may not be able to develop the same attitude toward the characters as the author claims to have and so may be imperfectly cognizant of their potentialities for "liberation." But of course Oates's statement, like any comment upon a literary text, is reductive, minimizing the total effect the character will make on a reader. She must certainly know on some level, as her readers do, that it is debilitation not liberation which is usually the more salient impression made by her characters.

This failure of the characters to suggest convincingly that they are capable of transcendence may be related to another problem—their credibility. For example, the ebullience of Jules in *them*—so valued by the author—may not be compelling to the reader. Another such unconvincing character for many readers is Elena of *Do With Me What You Will*, who is portrayed as a vacuous Sleeping Beauty who awakens to selfhood through orgasm. Some readers find it hard to care about or to believe in a character who seems to lack all reality, however appropriate her "selflessness" may be for the orgasmic release which breathes life into her. In other words, Oates's characters sometimes fail to coalesce as credible creations or fail to arouse the reader's empathy and concern. This is not to underestimate the scores of characters who are vividly realized—drawn with compassion and insight—throughout Oates's fiction. Yet she also has a host of bizarre, uncompelling characters. While one cannot ask that a writer create "likeable" characters with whom one can "identify," nonetheless one can ask that the writer evoke their feelings and present their problems skillfully enough so that one feels some compulsion to continue reading about them. I am not the only reader to complain that *The Assassins*, for example, in spite of its rich symbolic and thematic complexity, is very nearly an unreadable book,[13] and a large measure of the problem is that it is hard to care about any of the Petries.

That some of the short stories are unsatisfying is due less often to their lack of credibility than it is to their thematic and formal shapelessness. One can believe in the emotional distress of the women of "I Was in Love" and "Unmailed, Unwritten Letters" (both in *The Wheel of Love*), but one cannot gain any perspective on it. Oates has merely recorded the raw experiences; she has not worked them into "hypotheses" or "complex propositions" about the nature of experience. The experimental techniques employed in many of these stories do not compensate for their annoying rhetorical irresolution. It may well be Oates's aim to maintain this open-endedness, as some commentators have suggested,[14] but in my opinion such stories, in addition to withholding any sort of catharsis for the reader, do not display Oates's craftsmanship at its best. On the other hand, stories like "First Views of the Enemy " *(Upon the Sweeping Flood)*, "Pastoral Blood" *(By the North Gate)*, "In the Region of Ice" *(The Wheel of Love)*, "Where Are You Going, Where Have You Been?" *(The Wheel of Love)*, "Magna Mater" *(The Goddess)*, and others profit from masterful control, precision, and economy of rendering, as well as thematic luminosity. In her novels, however, Oates is more likely to lapse into stylistic weaknesses.

The larger canvas of the novel sometimes allows her to indulge in a lamentable verbosity. One wishes that she would shape and prune the monotonous and excessive verbiage. Very often staccatolike phrases and sentences saying essentially the same thing follow one another in rapid succession, as in this quite typical passage from the Yvonne section of *The Assassins*: "—wanted only for it to end, to end. She wanted only for it to end. For everything to end. Now that she knew, now that she knew why they were here, why Andrew had died, now that she knew as if from the inside these strangers with their individual faces, this crowd of voices . . . now that she knew them . . . how could anything endure it, such a carnival? . . . now that she understood, she wanted only for it to end" (p. 428). While the style, as in this passage, may be an attempted echo of the character's obsessions, one could get the point with less reiteration. The reader is likely to retreat with annoyance rather than to be drawn into the mood of the character or to engage himself in a serious consideration of the hypothetical propositions which Oates is offering for his perusal. Oates, like D. H. Lawrence and others who attempt to describe the indescribable—the inchoate emotional experiences of human beings, sometimes taxes excessively the descriptive power of language. Her profusive writing tends to smother rather than to evoke the intended emotional effect.

But a more important cause than unconvincing characterization or unpolished style for the sometimes flawed rhetoric of Oates's novels may be that the realistic novel is too clumsy a vehicle for her modernist formulation and assessment of the problems of selfhood and for the private vision she posits. Because Oates's novels are, as she says, "grounded in the density of existential life,"[15] one is likely to respond more directly to the *reality* of Jules's murder of the policeman in *them* than to its symbolic ramifications as spiritual rebirth; conversely, one is likely to be more troubled by the credibility of Elena's Sleeping-Beauty character in *Do With Me What You Will* than to be taken with the figurative appropriateness of it for her unliberated self. A reader would perhaps be more able to respond to Oates's visionary hypotheses if they were more clearly presented as fictional constructs rather than as what they appear to be, naturalistic case studies. For example, another visionary, Flannery O'Connor—by breaking with the realistic mode in her art of the grotesque—prepares us to accept the often apocalyptic transformations of her characters. But Oates has been committed to her own kind of realistic fiction which she characterizes as a "synthesis of the 'existential' and the 'timeless.' " She adds, "I believe that writing should re-create a world, sanctifying the real world by honoring its complexities."[16] But "the complexities of the real world" may not so readily accommodate and so easily synthesize with the "timeless" truths of Oates's monistic vision. Furthermore, perhaps the naturalistic tradition within which Oates often seems to be writing has built into it expectations of meaning at odds with her vision. The form creates meaning—it prepares for a deterministic perspective— in spite of the different meaning the author tries to affix to it. If *them* is persistently read *straight* rather than as the parody of the naturalistic novel which Oates claims it is intended to be, perhaps the profuse detailing of external reality gets in the way of Oates's central concern with the internal emotional lives of her characters and their possibilities for liberating transcendence.

Maybe this is why in her two most recent novels, *The Assassins* and *Childwold*, Oates experiments with spatial rather than narrative order and uses interior monologue and stream-of-consciousness techniques. Perhaps she is striving for greater correlation between the fragmented lives of her characters and the form of the novel, presenting them by grounding her novels more centrally within the characters' consciousness. But Oates is not always skillful in rendering subjective states directly. On the whole I find stories and portions of novels thus related much less successful than others because the style encourages Oates's tendency toward excessive repetition. Locked in their various neuroses, psychoses, and depressions, her characters often dwell interminably and insufferably upon their obsessions. Furthermore, the danger Oates encounters as an experimentalist, vividly illustrated in *The Assassins*, is that the elaborately crafted novel may seem strained and contrived, lacking that sense of experiential reality which she can sometimes re-create vividly. Nonetheless, the skillfully interwoven voices of *Childwold* portend well for her ability to develop novelistic techniques, forms, and style increasingly harmonious with her visionary perspective.

The radically experimental style and structure of Oates's two recent novels suggest that in the future she may well abandon entirely the conventional narrative techniques which have typified her earlier fiction. Perhaps she senses that this is the direction in which she must move in order to synthesize her method with her increasingly explicit preoccupation with the intangible interconnectedness of the self and "the other," for there is no doubt that her later work is much less grounded in external realistic experience than her earlier pieces. The way out of a constricted and fragmented self is less often posited in terms of violent or sexual consummation, more often through a kind of transcendence of the bodily self and personal ego, as, for example, in *The Assassins* the egoless serenity of Stephen Petrie, and in *Childwold* the oneness with the flow of life force felt momentarily by Laney Bartlett and more consistently by her grandfather, and the ascetic oneness attempted by Kasch. Futhermore, in addition to that strange volume of short stories, *The Poisoned Kiss*, which records bizarre confrontations of the self and "the other" and which Oates claims to have "translated" from an imaginary author in a kind of mystical trance, her most recent collection of short stories, *Night-Side*, depicts characters who through extra-sensory perception, intuition, strange experiences, chance happenings, and the like, experience intimations of a spiritually interconnected universe which sometimes call into question the very postulation of the self as a separate, mortal phenomenon. Oates's next novel, *The Son of the Morning*, not yet released at this writing, allegedly centers on religious experience and promises to be an even more explicit exploration of the visionary.

While all artists have to balance their Coleridgean primary and secondary imaginations, this balancing is an especially delicate problem for Joyce Carol Oates. Her appeal to a large audience, I suspect, lies predominantly in her function as a "medium" of our culture who duplicates its obsessions, neuroses, and violence. With about five million of her books currently in print, she has apparently tapped some visceral "resevoir of energy" in American experience; she does perhaps "articulate the very worst" so that it "can be dealt with and not simply feared." A voice of the communal consciousness of our culture, she has a talent to be respected and nurtured. More than likely, however, her increasingly explicit visionary concerns and her increasingly experimental techniques will lessen her popularity with a mass audience, but she will perhaps in these terms, rather than in the more conventional modes of her earlier fiction work out a more credible aesthetic synthesis of the "existential" and the "timeless," for none of her novels, it seems to me, is yet equal to the very best fiction of our era.

Joyce Carol Oates's many flawless, memorable short stories secure her position as an important writer in the history of American letters. Her bold and insightful critical essays and reviews offer revealing perspectives on her own views and craftsmanship as well as on those of others. Moreover, her several volumes of poetry (and to a lesser degree her four plays), which I have not had the space to discuss in this study, are important facets of her total work, because, to a very high degree, "everything is related" in her widely ranging canon, as Oates herself recognizes. She characterizes her poems as "lyric expressions of larger, dramatic, emotional predicaments, and they belong to fully-developed fictional characters who 'exist' else-where."[17] The poems, then, like the essays, are revealing indexes to the stories and novels. If I have expressed some disappointment that her novels—fascinating as they are—are not completely reso-nant, it is because I admire the seriousness and acuteness with which she relentlessly probes the nature of contemporary human experi-ence and because I am convinced that she has a prodigious talent, coupled with enormous energy and dedication to her craft, which could yet make her a most significant voice in the fiction of our era.

Notes and References

Chapter One

1. "Transformations of Self: An Interview with Joyce Carol Oates," *Ohio Review*, 15, i (1973), 54.
2. Joe David Bellamy, "The Dark Lady of American Letters," *Atlantic*, 229 (February 1972), 67.
3. Walter Clemons, "Joyce Carol Oates: Love and Violence," *Newsweek*, December 11, 1972, p. 73.
4. Ibid., pp. 72–73.
5. "Other Celebrity Voices: How Art Has Touched Our Lives," *Today's Health*, 52 (May 1974), 31.
6. R. M. Adams, "Joyce Carol Oates at Home," *New York Times Book Review*, September 28, 1969, p. 48.
7. Bellamy, p. 66.
8. Clemons, p. 73.
9. Ibid., p. 74.
10. Letter to the author, February 23, 1976.
11. "Transformations of Self," p. 55.
12. Interview with the author, May 25, 1976.
13. "The Myth of the Isolated Artist," *Psychology Today*, 6 (May 1973), 74–75.
14. *New Heaven, New Earth: The Visionary Experience in Literature* (New York, 1974), p. 260.
15. "The Myth of the Isolated Artist."
16. In the essay "The Hostile Sun: The Poetry of D. H. Lawrence," Oates sympathizes with Lawrence's detestation of the goal of psychoanalysis: "The Aristotelian-Freudian-'classicist' model of psychological health—that emotions be purged, refined, made totally conscious and therefore discharged of their power—is certainly a dubious one. . . . Such a model assumes the malevolent nature of the 'id'; from this is a simple step to the assumption that the 'id' is a natural enemy of 'civilization.' . . . *Why* must so much of human behavior be classified as 'neurotic' when in fact it is simply natural, given certain personalities and certain environments? The impulse to 'make well' may be the most sinister of Western civilization's goals" (*New Heaven, New Earth*, pp. 72–73).
17. *The Edge of Impossibility: Tragic Forms in Literature*, Greenwich, Conn., 1973, pp. 8, 165–92.
18. "New Heaven and New Earth," *Saturday Review*, November 4, 1972, pp. 52–53.

19. *New Heaven, New Earth,* pp. 6, 194, 179.

20. "The Death Throes of Romanticism: The Poetry of Sylvia Plath," *New Heaven, New Earth,* pp. 114, 140.

21. Ibid., pp. 126–27.

22. "Anarchy and Order in Beckett's Trilogy," *New Heaven, New Earth,* pp. 94–95.

23. "Ionesco's Dances of Death," *The Edge of Impossibility,* p. 215.

24. "Joyce Carol Oates on Thoreau's *Walden,*" *Mademoiselle,* April 1973, pp. 96, 98.

25. "New Heaven and New Earth," pp. 53–54.

26. "The Short Story," *Southern Humanities Review,* 5 (Summer 1971), 213–14.

27. "The Myth of the Isolated Artist."

28. *New Heaven, New Earth,* p. 284.

29. "The Myth of the Isolated Artist."

30. *New Heaven, New Earth,* p. 7.

31. "The Myth of the Isolated Artist."

32. Clemons, p. 73.

33. Bellamy, p. 64.

34. Letter to the author, October 22, 1975.

35. *New Heaven, New Earth,* pp. 37-81.

36. *Writer,* June 1966, 44.

37. "The Myth of the Isolated Artist."

38. "New Heaven and New Earth," p. 54.

39. *New Heaven, New Earth,* p. 46.

Chapter Two

1. *By the North Gate* (Greenwich, Conn., 1971). Page references are cited in the text.

2. *Upon the Sweeping Flood* (Greenwich, Conn., 1972). Page references are cited in the text.

3. *With Shuddering Fall* (Greenwich, Conn., 1971). Page references are cited in the text.

4. J. Preston Cole, *The Problematic Self in Kierkegaard and Freud* (New Haven and London, 1971), pp. 97–98.

5. *Selected Poems of George Meredith,* ed. Graham Hough (London, 1962), p. 55.

6. "The Birth of Tragedy," *Basic Writings of Nietzsche,* ed. Walter Kaufmann (New York, 1968), p. 257.

Chapter Three

1. Linda Kuehl, ed., "An Interview with Joyce Carol Oates," *Commonweal,* 91 (December 5, 1969), 308.

2. *A Garden of Earthly Delights* (Greenwich, Conn., 1974). Page references are cited in the text.

3. "Joyce Carol Oates and an Old Master," *Critique*, 15, i (1973), 48-58.

4. *Expensive People* (Greenwich, Conn., 1974). Page references are cited in the text.

5. *The Rise of the Novel* (Berkeley, 1971), p. 32.

6. Perhaps the supposed allusion is to Lady MacBeth's vivid declaration in Act I, VII, 54–59:

> I have given suck, and know
> How tender 'tis to love the babe that milks me:
> I would, while it was smiling in my face,
> Have pluck'd my nipple from his boneless gums,
> And dash'd the brains out, had I so sworn as you
> Have done to this.

7. "Author Oates has but one message in her demonic little tale: behind the suburban facade lie corruption and madness. To hear her tell it, American husbands and wives are nice clean-cut vampires planting stakes in each other's hearts. And there is always the monster in the playroom" ("The Doomed and the Damned," *Time*, November 1, 1968, p. 102).

8. *them* (Greenwich, Conn., 1970). Page references are cited in the text.

9. Interview with the author, May 25, 1976.

10. John L'Heureux, "Mirage-Seekers," *Atlantic*, October 1969, p. 129.

11. Oates's own striking term from "The Tragedy of Existence: Shakespeare's *Troilus and Cressida*," *The Edge of Impossibility*, p. 27.

12. Reviewers have almost universally viewed the riot as a totally destructive occurrence, emblematic of the meaningless violence and emotion in the novel as a whole: "Emotions in this world are superficial, temporary, and violent; they don't really 'express' anything, and behind their emptiness one feels flowering an impulse toward the meaningless, consuming violence of the 1967 riots in Detroit." Robert M. Adams, "Them," *New York Times Book Review*, September 28, 1969, p. 4. In so doing, they have missed the affirmation implicit in this ironically liberating violence: "Nothing can come from nothing, no energy from a bodiless spirit; thus, there can be no violence out of a sense of nothing, for violence is always an affirmation" (Oates, *The Edge of Impossibility*, p. 11).

13. "In *them*, I saw Jules as a kind of American success in an ironic sense, of course. He is a hero and a murderer at once. I think that is ironic. I hope it is." (Kuehl, p. 308).

14. In claiming that Oates depicts an unchangeable "kernel of the self," I differ both with John Gardner ("Conversations with John Gardner on Writers and Writing," *Detroit Magazine, Detroit Free Press*, March 23, 1975, p. 20), who claims that "Joyce believes that people wander into your life, accidents happen constantly, and there is no sort of 'core of being' " and Constance

Ayers Denne ("Joyce Carol Oates's Women," *The Nation*, 219 [December 7, 1974], 597), who claims that Oates presents selfhood as a process of continual growth: "The truly human life requires continual growth, which in turn depends upon the individual's ability to integrate new experiences into the total personality."

15. James R. Giles, "Suffering, Transcendence, and Artistic Form: Joyce Carol Oates's *them*," *Arizona Quarterly*, 32 (Autumn 1976), 225.

Chapter Four

. 1. The title page of the novel includes this dedication: "This book is for all of us who pursue the phantasmagoria of personality."

2. *Wonderland* (Greenwich, Conn., 1973). Page references are cited in the text.

3. *Wonderland* (New York, 1971), p. 512.

4. In the revision of the novel, Oates not only rewrote the ending, significantly shortening it and profoundly altering the final impression of Jesse, she dropped an introductory tableau prefiguring the final scene in which a nameless, sexless childlike figure (Shelley) desperately runs from a man (Jesse).

5. Nonetheless, in a letter to the author, October 22, 1975, Oates claims: "The paperback edition's ending of WONDERLAND is the definitive one. The reason behind my changing the ending—at great trouble needless to say, to my publisher and myself—is too complicated to go into, and too personal." Elsewhere, in "Art: Therapy and Magic," *American Journal*, 1 (July 3, 1973), 17–21, she claims that she changed it because in the original, she consciously and mistakenly resisted her "intuition."

6. "New Heaven and New Earth," p. 53.

7. Bellamy, p. 64.

8. Donald Rackin, "Alice's Journey to the End of Night," *Aspects of Alice: Lewis Carroll's Dreamchild as Seen through Critics' Looking-Glasses, 1865–1975*, ed. Robert Phillips (New York, 1971), pp. 392–93.

9. William Empson, "Alice in Wonderland: The Child as Swain," *Alice's Adventures in Wonderland: A Critical Handbook*, ed. Donald Rackin (Belmont, Calif., 1969), pp. 251–52.

10. I am indebted to a student, Vito Peraino, who first called attention to Oates's parallel.

11. Erik H. Erikson, "The Theory of Infantile Sexuality," *Childhood and Society*, (New York, 1963), pp. 48–108.

12. See particularly, Géza Róheim, from "Further Insights," and Paul Schilder, "Psychoanalytic Remarks on *Alice in Wonderland* and Lewis Carroll," both in *Aspects of Alice*, pp. 332–39, 283–92.

13. "I think Carroll must have been dealing partly with the notion of the Darwinian game, the struggle for survival, that we're all playing a great game of chess, and in the Darwinian struggle people and creatures eat one another.

There's so much eating, that is why the *Alice* books are very frightening for children. Maybe some of you remember reading them as children, and perhaps you were frightened by them. There's so much about eating and metamorphosis." Oates speaking after a poetry reading at the Conference on Modern Literature, East Lansing, Michigan, October 14, 1977.

14. Ellen Friedman, "Joyce Carol Oates's *Wonderland:* The Journey from 'I' to 'Eye,' " unpublished essay read at MLA Convention, December 1977.

15. I should note, however, that Jesse's obsession with being watched over by various "fathers," and even by a "true, pure, undefiled" self, makes Cheshire-Cat presences ubiquitous in his Wonderland.

16. Rackin, p. 414.

17. Ibid., pp., 414–15.

18. "Today's 'Wonder-World' Needs Alice," *Aspects of Alice*, pp. 3–12.

19. The poem, originally entitled "Iris into Eye," was published as Oates's own in *Poetry Northwest*, Autumn 1970.

20. *Do With Me What You Will* (Greenwich, Conn., 1974). Page references are cited in the text.

21. This incident is almost certainly based on Arville D. Garland's murder of his seventeen-year-old daughter, Sandra, and three of her friends on May 8, 1970, for which he was found guilty of manslaughter and second-degree murder and sentenced to 10–40 years by Detroit Recorder's Court Judge Joseph A. Gillis, a case which received much local publicity.

22. The Mered Dawe case is based loosely on that of John A. Sinclair, White Panther leader, who was sentenced on July 28, 1969, to nine and one-half to ten years for possession of marijuana by Detroit Recorder's Court Judge Robert J. Colombo. He was found guilty of giving two marijuana cigarettes to undercover police officers on December 22, 1966. Both Sinclair and his attorney, Justin C. Ravitz, argued that Sinclair was set up by the police because of his anti-establishment political activism. The case received publicity for a number of years.

Chapter Five

1. *New Heaven, New Earth*, p. 260.

2. Oates explained this in an interview with the author, May 25, 1976.

3. *The Assassins* (New York, 1975). Page references are cited in the text.

4. "The symbol of the cosmic tree rooted in this world and growing up to heaven" is both "man" and "the way of life itself, a growing into that which eternally is and does not change; which springs from the union of opposites and, by its eternal presence, also makes that union possible." "Psychological Aspects of the Mother Archetype," *Collected Works of C. G. Jung*, trans. R. F. C. Hull, 9, i (London, 1959), p. 110.

5. "The Psychology of the Child Archetype," Ibid., p. 162.

6. Oates suggests the latter in an interview with the author, May 25, 1976.

7. This multivarious symbol, the uroboros—the circular snake biting its tail—seems to be used by Oates to portray the terrible aspects of the feminine archetype embodied in Yvonne. See Erich Neumann, *The Great Mother* (New York, 1955), pp. 18, 170.

8. In Jungian terms she fails to take the first vital step in the process of individuation, confrontation with the shadow: "The shadow is a moral problem that challenges the whole ego-personality, for no one can become conscious of the shadow without considerable moral effort. To become conscious of it involves recognizing the dark aspects of the personality as present and real. This act is the essential condition for any kind of self-knowledge, and it therefore, as a rule, meets with considerable resistance." C. G. Jung, *Aion: Researches into the Phenomenology of the Self*, trans. R. F. C. Hull (Princeton, 1968), p. 8.

9. The process "by which a person becomes a psychological 'individual,' that is, a separate, indivisible unity or 'whole' " by synthesizing unconscious process with the conscious ego. "Conscious, Unconscious, and Individuation," *Collected Works of C. G. Jung*, 9, i: 275.

10. See "Christ, A Symbol of the Self," *Aion*, pp. 36–71.

11. Jung defines *anima* as an archetypal personification of the unconscious in a man which is invariable a *female* figure. "The Syzygy: Anima and Animus," Ibid., pp. 11–22.

12. See "The Sign of the Fishes," "The Historical Significance of the Fish," "The Ambivalence of the Fish Symbol," "The Fish in Alchemy," and "The Alchemical Interpretation of the Fish," Ibid., pp. 72–94, 103–72.

13. Ibid., p. 27.

14. "It must be reckoned a psychic catastrophe when the *ego is assimilated by the self.* . . . It is of the greatest importance that the ego should be anchored in the world of consciousness. . . . Reality . . . [has] to be protected against an archaic, 'eternal' and 'ubiquitous' dream state." Ibid., pp. 24–25.

15. In a letter to the author, February 23, 1976.

16. *Childwold* (New York, 1976). Page references are cited in the text.

Chapter Six

1. *The Wheel of Love and Other Stories* (Greenwich, Conn., 1972). Page references are cited in the text.

2. This point is convincingly developed in Joyce W. Wegs, " 'Don't You Know Who I Am?': The Grotesque in Oates's 'Where Are You Going, Where Have You Been?'," *Journal of Narrative Technique*, 5 (January 1975), 66–72.

3. Oates confirms in a letter to Professor Arnold Goldsmith that this story grew out of her relationship in 1965 with a student, Richard Wishnetsky, at the University of Detroit, who later (February 12, 1966) shot and killed Rabbi Morris Adler and himself in front of Shaaray Zedek synagogue in Detroit. Oates's fascinating personal reminiscence of her student, "Richard

Wishnetsky: Joyce Oates Supplies a Missing View," was published in *Detroit Magazine, Detroit Free Press* (March 6, 1966).

4. Oates confirms that Kali is the goddess implied in the title in a letter to the author, October 22, 1975: "Kali is the specific 'goddess' of the title, but the collection deals with other manifestations of the 'goddess'—that is, the image of women in both men's and women's imaginations. Most of the stories turn upon the unconscious or partly-conscious manifestations of the feminine archetype in the character; in a story like 'Magna Mater,' the dominant psychic content isn't realized by the character but by the reader. . . . Our lives are largely guided by unconscious contents and when those contents were given clear, definable titles—the 'gods' and 'goddesses' of antiquity—it was at least easier to know when one was under their enchantment. Today in a secularized world, we fall under the power of various psychic contents and fail to realize that they are altering our lives, or even that they exist. This is the price we pay for our 'rationality.' "

5. *The Goddess and Other Women* (New York, 1974). Page references are cited in the text.

6. *The Hungry Ghosts: Seven Allusive Comedies* (Los Angeles, 1974). Page references are cited in the text.

7. Two additional stories, "The Transformation of Vincent Scoville" and "The Liberation of Jake Hanley," set at Hilberry and told with the same heavy satire, are collected in the recently published volume, *Crossing the Border* (New York, 1976).

8. Bellamy, p. 64.

9. Clemons, p. 77.

10. It appeared under this title in *New American Review*, November 1971.

11. *Marriages and Infidelities* (Greenwich, Conn., 1973). Page references are cited in the text.

12. Interestingly, just as Joyce has commented that Gabriel Conroy is the kind of person he might have become had he stayed in Ireland, Oates has said that Ilena is "a way I could have gone" (Clemons, p. 74).

13. Other similarly allusive stories in this volume include "Turn of the Screw," in which one of the turns of the screw may be literary parallels to Thomas Mann's "Death in Venice" as well as Henry James's famous story. This typographically unusual story—dual journalistic accounts in parallel columns on the page—is, according to Oates, "a kind of parody of journal-keeping . . . intense and rigorous self-analysis that, despite its puritanical thoroughness, leads the protagonists deeper into illusion." Nonetheless, "the delusion won't seriously matter since it will be turned into art. The young man, misread by the artist, will nevertheless inspire him to create one of his most powerful and mysterious novellas" (letter to the author, February 23, 1976). In this letter she also acknowledges that "Nightmusic," the final story in the volume, "is loosely based on Mozart's life—very loosely," and adds: "I've done a sequence of similar works, usually about old or older men who have achieved some success in their fields. The most recent is 'The

Sacrifice,' in FICTION INTERNATIONAL. 'Knowing,' based (again, loosely) on Charles Sanders Peirce will come out in ONTARIO REVIEW this spring, and I'm completing a story suggested by Joyce (James, that is) and his daughter, a story without a title."

14. "Afterword," *The Poisoned Kiss and Other Stories from the Portuguese* (New York, 1975). Page references are cited in the text.

Chapter Seven

1. "The Nightmare of Naturalism: Harriette Arnow's *The Dollmaker*, *New Heaven, New Earth*, pp. 97–110.
2. See, for example, Mary Kathryn Grant, R. S. M., *The Tragic Vision of Joyce Carol Oates* (Durham, N.C., 1978), who documents the physical and rhetorical violence in Oates's work and who can find very little affirmation beyond sheer "getting through."
3. Letter to Dale Boesky, "Correspondence with Miss Joyce Carol Oates," *International Review of Psychoanalysis*, 2 (1975), 482.
4. "Preface," *Where Are You Going, Where Have You Been?: Stories of Young America* (Greenwich, Conn., 1974), p. 10.
5. "The Man on the Quaker Oats Box: Characteristics of Recent Experimental Fiction," *Georgia Review*, 20 (Fall 1972), 300.
6. "*Ulysses*, Order, and Myth," *Dial*, 75 (November 1923), 480.
7. *New Heaven, New Earth*, p. 4.
8. Boesky, p. 484.
9. Kuehl, p. 308.
10. Boesky, p. 483.
11. "Lawrence's Götterdämmerung: The Tragic Vision of *Women in Love*," *Critical Inquiry*, 4 (Spring 1978), p. 564.
12. Boesky, p. 482.
13. See, for example, Jim Neubacher, "Violence: Some Sadism in 2 Cool Novels," *Detroit Free Press*, December 28, 1975, p. 5-B.
14. See, for example, Gail Godwin, "An Oates Scrapbook," *North American Review*, 256 (Winter 1971–72), 67–70.
15. "Afterword," *The Poisoned Kiss*, p. 187.
16. Ibid., pp. 187–88.
17. "Transformations of Self," p. 50.

Selected Bibliography

PRIMARY SOURCES

1. Novels and Novella
The Assassins. New York: Vanguard Press, 1975. Paperback reprint, Greenwich, Conn.: Fawcett, 1976.
Childwold. New York: Vanguard Press, 1976.
Do With Me What You Will. New York: Vanguard Press, 1973. Paperback reprint, Greenwich, Conn.: Fawcett, 1974.
Expensive People. New York: Vanguard Press, 1968. Paperback reprint, Greenwich, Conn.: Fawcett, 1974.
A Garden of Earthly Delights. New York: Vanguard Press, 1967. Paperback reprint, Greenwich, Conn.: Fawcett, 1969.
The Son of the Morning. New York: Vanguard Press, 1978 (forthcoming).
them. New York: Vanguard Press, 1969. Paperback reprint: Greenwich, Conn.: Fawcett, 1970.
The Triumph of the Spider Monkey. Los Angeles: Black Sparrow Press, 1976. A novella.
With Shuddering Fall. New York: Vanguard Press, 1964. Paperback reprint, Greenwich, Conn.: Fawcett, 1971.
Wonderland. New York: Vanguard Press, 1971. Paperback reprint, Greenwich, Conn.: Fawcett, 1973.

2. Collected Short Stories
All the Good People I've Left Behind. Santa Barbara: Black Sparrow Press, 1978 (forthcoming).
By the North Gate. New York: Vanguard Press, 1963. Paperback reprint, Greenwich, Conn.: Fawcett, 1971.
Crossing the Border. New York: Vanguard Press, 1976.
The Goddess and Other Women. New York: Vanguard Press, 1974. Paperback reprint, Greenwich, Conn.: Fawcett, 1976.
The Hungry Ghosts: Seven Allusive Comedies. Los Angeles: Black Sparrow Press, 1974.
Marriages and Infidelities. New York: Vanguard Press, 1972. Paperback reprint, Greenwich, Conn.: Fawcett, 1973.
Night-Side. New York: Vanguard Press, 1977.
The Poisoned Kiss and Other Stories from the Portuguese, by "Fernandes." New York: Vanguard Press, 1975.

The Seduction and Other Stories. Los Angeles: Black Sparrow Press, 1975.
Upon the Sweeping Flood and Other Stories. New York: Vanguard Press,
    1966. Paperback reprint, Greenwich, Conn.: Fawcett, 1971.
The Wheel of Love and Other Stories. New York: Vanguard Press, 1970.
    Paperback reprint, Greenwich, Conn.: Fawcett, 1971.
Where Are You Going? Where Have You Been? Stories of Young America.
    Greenwich, Conn.: Fawcett, 1974. A paperback collection.

3. Collected Poems
Angel Fire. Baton Rouge: Louisiana State University Press, 1973.
Anonymous Sins and Other Poems. Baton Rouge: Louisiana State University
    Press, 1969.
Dreaming America and Other Poems. [N.P.]: Aloe Editions, 1973.
The Fabulous Beasts. Baton Rouge: Louisiana State University Press, 1975.
Love and Its Derangements. Baton Rouge: Louisiana State University Press,
    1970.
Love and Its Derangements and Other Poems (includes *Love and Its
    Derangements, Angel Face,* and *Anonymous Sins and Other Poems*).
    Greenwich, Conn.: Fawcett, 1974.
Women in Love and Other Poems. New York: Albondocani Press, 1968.
Women Whose Lives are Food, Men Whose Lives are Money. Baton Rouge:
    Louisiana State University Press, 1978.

4. Essays
The Edge of Impossibility: Tragic Forms in Literature. New York: Vanguard
    Press, 1972. Paperback reprint, Greenwich, Conn.: Fawcett, 1973.
The Hostile Sun: The Poetry of D. H. Lawrence. Los Angeles: Black Sparrow
    Press, 1973 (reprinted in *New Heaven, New Earth*).
New Heaven, New Earth: The Visionary Experience in Literature. New York:
    Vanguard Press, 1974.

5. Miscellany
Cupid and Psyche. New York: Albondocani Press, 1970. A single story,
    reprinted as "The Dreaming Woman" in *The Seduction.*
Daisy. Santa Barbara: Black Sparrow Press, 1977. A single story, reprinted in
    Night-Side.
The Girl. Cambridge, Mass.: Pomegranate Press, 1974. A single story,
    reprinted in *The Goddess.*
In Case of Accidental Death. Cambridge, Mass.: Pomegranate Press, 1972.
Miracle Play. Los Angeles: Black Sparrow Press, 1974. A play.
Public Outcry. Pittsburgh: Slow Loris Press, 1976. A broadside.
Scenes from American Life: Contemporary Short Fiction. New York: Random
    House, 1972. An anthology edited by Oates.
Wooded Forms. New York: Albondocani Press, 1972. A single poem.

6. Uncollected Essays (a selected list)

"The Art of Eudora Welty," *Shenandoah,* 20, iii (1969), 54–57.

"Art: Therapy and Magic," *American Journal,* 1 (July 3, 1973), 17–21.

"Background and Foreground in Fiction," *Writer,* August 1967, pp. 11–13.

"Building Tension in the Short Story," *Writer,* June 1966, pp. 11–12, 44.

"The Comedy of Metamorphosis in the *Revenger's Tragedy,*" *Bucknell Review,* 11 (December 1962), 38–52.

"Disguised Fiction," *PMLA,* 89 (May 1974), 580–81.

"The Existential Comedy of Conrad's 'Youth,' " *Renascence,* 26 (Fall 1963), 22–28.

"The 'Fifth Act' and the Chorus in the English and Scottish Ballads," *Dalhousie Review,* 42 (Autumn 1962), 119–29.

" 'The Immense Indifference of Things': The Tragedy of Conrad's *Nostromo,*" *Novel: A Forum on Fiction,* 9 (Fall 1975), 5–22.

"Is This the Promised End?: The Tragedy of King Lear," *Journal of Aesthetics and Art Criticism,* 33 (Fall 1974), 19–32.

"Jocoserious Joyce," *Critical Inquiry,* 2 (Summer 1976), 677–88.

"Joyce Carol Oates on Thoreau's *Walden,*" *Mademoiselle,* April 1973, pp. 96, 98.

"Lawrence's *Götterdämmerung:* The Tragic Vision of *Women in Love,*" *Critical Inquiry,* 4 (Spring 1978), 559–78.

"Man Under Sentence of Death: The Novels of James M. Cain," *Tough Guy Writers of the Thirties,* ed. David Madden. Carbondale: Southern Illinois University Press, 1968, pp. 110–28.

"Masquerade and Marriage: Fielding's Comedies of Identity," *Ball State University Forum,* 6 (Autumn, 1965), 10–21.

"The Myth of the Isolated Artist," *Psychology Today,* 6 (May 1973), 74–75.

"New Heaven and New Earth," *Saturday Review,* November 4, 1972, pp. 51–54. Reprinted in *Arts in Society,* 10 (1973), 36–43.

"Out of the Machine," *Atlantic,* July 1971, pp. 42–45.

"A Personal View of Nabokov," *Saturday Review of the Arts,* January 1973, pp. 36–37.

"Porter's 'Noon Wine': A Stifled Tragedy," *Renascence,* 27 (Spring 1965), 157–62.

"The Short Story," *Southern Humanities Review,* 5 (Summer 1971), 213–14.

"The Unique/Universal in Fiction," *Writer,* January 1973, pp. 9–12.

"Updike's American Comedies," *Modern Fiction Studies,* 21 (Autumn 1975), 549–72.

SECONDARY SOURCES

1. Critical Essays and Interviews

ADAMS, R. M. "Joyce Carol Oates at Home," *New York Times Book Review,* September 28, 1969, pp. 4–5, 48. Brief but informative interview-article.

ALLEN, BRUCE. "Intrusions of Consciousness," *Hudson Review*, 28 (Winter 1975–76), 611–15. This review-article about *New Heaven, New Earth* claims "visionary" is never perfectly clear and that the organization of the book is "very loose," yet finds fascinating Oates's mixing up of "acute critical analyses with heady speculation and challenging (often critically revealing) digressions."

ALLEN, MARY I. "The Terrified Women of Joyce Carol Oates," *The Necessary Blankness: Women in Major American Fiction of the Sixties*. Urbana: University of Illinois Press, 1976, pp. 133–59. This critical study finds Oates to be a master at depicting women's blankness and pervasive terror—of men, sexuality, motherhood, violence, lack of control.

ANDERSEN, SALLY. "The Poetry of Joyce Carol Oates," *Spirit*, 39 (Fall 1972), 24–29. This review article about *Love and Its Derangements* claims that some poems abound in vague emotion and empty verbiage, some have stale and illogical metaphors, and some probe successfully the deeply moving themes of the novels.

AVANT, JOHN ALFRED. "An Interview with Joyce Carol Oates," *Library Journal*, (November 15, 1972), 3711–12. This brief interview probes Oates's literary views and plans.

BATTERBERRY, MICHAEL and ARIANE, eds. "Focus on Joyce Carol Oates," *Harper's Bazaar*, September 1973, pp. 159, 174, 176. Oates responds to questions specifically about *Do With Me What You Will* and generally about her views on the nature and function of the law.

BELLAMY, JOE DAVID, ed. "The Dark Lady of American Letters: An Interview with Joyce Carol Oates," *Atlantic*, February 1972, pp. 63–67. (Reprinted in *The New Fiction: Interviews with Innovative American Writers* Urbana: University of Illinois Press, 1974.) Edited correspondence; thoughtful, extended responses to the interviewer's questions about writing habits and views on fiction specifically and generally.

BENDER, EILEEN T. "The Artistic Vision, Theory and Practice of Joyce Carol Oates," unpublished Ph.D. dissertation, University of Notre Dame, 1977. Examining Oates's criticism and fiction, Bender focuses on the issue of "autonomy" shaping Oates's vision of self, society, and art.

—— "Autonomy and Influence: Joyce Carol Oates' *Marriage and Infidelities*," *Soundings*, 58 (Fall 1975), 390–406. This critical article discusses Oates's "fabulistic" reimaginings in "Turn of the Screw," "The Metamorphosis," "The Dead," and "The Sacred Marriage," which are "a dramatic critique of the myth of personal autonomy."

BOESKY, DALE. "Correspondence with Miss Joyce Carol Oates," *International Review of Psychoanalysis*, 2 (1975), 481–86. Two very long letters in which Oates responds specifically and generally to questions "which relate to the methodology of applied psychoanalysis and literature."

BURWELL, ROSE MARIE. "Joyce Carol Oates and an Old Master," *Critique:*

Essays in Modern Fiction, 15, i (1973), 48–58. Burwell convincingly argues that Oates drew the title and modeled the structure and imagery of *A Garden of Earthly Delights* on Hieronymous Bosch's sixteenth-century triptych.

———. "Joyce Carol Oates' First Novel," *Canadian Literature*, 73 (Summer 1977), 54–57. Burwell argues that the true subject of *With Shuddering Fall* is not madness or violence, but Jungian "individuation."

———. "The Process of Individuation as Narrative Structure: Joyce Carol Oates' *Do With Me What You Will*," *Critique: Studies in Modern Fiction*, 17, ii (1975), 93–106. The critic closely analyzes the novel's structure and Elena's successful synthesizing of personality in terms of Jungian states of individuation.

CLEMONS, WALTER. "Joyce Carol Oates: Love and Violence," *Newsweek*, December 11, 1972, pp. 72–74, 77. This appreciative essay based on an interview concludes that "Joyce Carol Oates belongs to that small group of writers who keep alive the central ambitions and energies of literature."

CREIGHTON, JOANNE V. "Joyce Carol Oates's Craftsmanship in *The Wheel of Love*," *Studies in Short Fiction*, 15 (Fall 1978). This article isolates characteristic features of Oates's short story craft, distinguishing the better stories from the less luminous.

———. "Unliberated Women in Joyce Carol Oates's Fiction," *World Literature Written in English*, 17 (April 1978), 165–75. Focusing on *Do With Me What You Will* and *The Goddess*, Creighton underscores the sexual roots of female nonliberation in Oates's fiction.

DALTON, ELIZABETH. "Joyce Carol Oates: Violence in the Head," *Commentary*, June 1970, pp. 75–77. This outspokenly critical review article argues that violence in *them* and earlier works is mainly in "the head" of the author, not convincingly worked into the fabric of the fiction; the result is a "failure of literary intelligence, of structure, and style," in which violence has an "oddly bland effect" on the reader without climax, tension, meaning, illumination, or credibility.

DENNE, CONSTANCE AYERS. "Joyce Carol Oates's Women," *Nation*, 219 (December 7, 1974), 597–99. This review article claims that Oates is as conscious of being a woman as an artist, then surveys Oates's women and suggests that Elena in *Do With Me What You Will* affirms "the possibility of liberation for all humankind from the restricting structures of the past."

DIKE, DONALD A. "The Aggressive Victim in the Fiction of Joyce Carol Oates," *Greyfriar*, 15 (1974), 13–29. Dike argues that Oates's major characters are typically "running away," fugitives in quest of a hypothetical freedom of pure self, but that most often they are locked in relationships to others which are characterized by mutual victimization and aggression.

DITSKY, JOHN. "The Man on the Quaker Oats Box: Characteristics of Recent

Experimental Fiction," *Georgia Review*, 26 (Fall 1972), 297–313. This review article places Oates with the experimentalists rather than realists "in spirit if not in form" because of her concern with "inner states" which are "the fragmented reflection . . . of the fragmented external world."

FOSSUM, ROBERT H. "Only Control: The Novels of Joyce Carol Oates," *Studies in the Novel*, 7 (Summer 1975), 285–97. Fossum argues that Oates's people "crave an order associated with 'home' and the loving father" which conflicts "with a yearning for the 'road' and freedom from the father" and "both are expressions of a struggle to control their own lives against the forces of 'accident,' circumstances, other people."

FRIEDMAN, ELLEN. " 'Dreaming America': The Fiction of Joyce Carol Oates," unpublished Ph.D. dissertation, New York University, 1978. Friedman places Oates's novels within the context of American culture, literary traditions, and ideals, seeing her characters bounded within a universe and society that they can "neither avoid, nor transcend, nor control."

GILES, JAMES R. "From Jimmy Gatz to Jules Wendall: A Study of 'Nothing Substantial'," *Dalhousie Review*, 56 (Winter 1976-77), 718–24. Paralleling Jules from *them* with Gatsby, Giles finds Oates's work a "respectful parody" of Fitzgerald's.

————. "The 'Marivaudian Being' Drowns his Children: Dehumanization in Donald Barthelme's 'Robert Kennedy Saved from Drowning' and Joyce Carol Oates' *Wonderland*," *Southern Humanities Review*, 9 (Winter 1975), 63–75. Giles finds that Barthelme's story and Oates's novel "present two views of the alienated and fragmented American of the sixties" who is equivalent to Poulet's "the Marvaudian being . . . a pastless futureless man, born anew at every moment."

————. " 'Suffering, Transcendence, and Artistic Form': Joyce Carol Oates's *them*," *Arizona Quarterly*, 32 (Autumn 1976), 213–26. The critic claims that the "tension between naturalistic documentation of struggle and pain and romantic glorification of the human soul is critical to *them*" and argues that Loretta is destroyed, Maureen saved, and Jules transformed from an "idealistic rebel to a calculating nihilist" in the course of the novel.

GODWIN, GAIL. "An Oates Scrapbook," *North American Review*, 256 (Winter 1971-72), 67-70. Godwin praises Oates's "deranging" of experience, the way her works evoke questions about the nature of human personality and refuse to supply definitive answers.

GRANT, MARY KATHRYN, R. S. M. *The Tragic Vision of Joyce Carol Oates*. Durham, N. C.: Duke University Press, 1978. Grant examines Oates's tragic vision, focusing on her thematic concern with violence and loss of community and her use of aesthetic and rhetorical violence.

HARTER, CAROL. "America as 'Consumer Garden': The Nightmare Vision of Joyce Carol Oates," *Revue des Langues Vivantes*, Bicentennial Issue

(1976), 171-87. Harter offers an insightful overview of the novels from *A Garden of Earthly Delights* through *Wonderland,* emphasizing the struggle of characters for liberation within the "consumer garden" of American society.

HODGE, MARION CECIL, JR. " 'What Moment Is Not Terrible': An Introduction to the Works of Joyce Carol Oates," unpublished Ph.D. dissertation, University of Tennessee, 1974. Hodge finds Oates's fiction a blend of realism and gothicism, her vision growing more optimistic, her novels brilliantly executed, and her poetry of poor quality.

KAZIN, ALFRED. "Oates," *Harper's,* August 1971, pp. 78–82. This impressionistic essay based on an interview characterizes Oates as haunted and obsessed with a "sweetly brutal sense of what American experience is really like" and argues that her fictionalizing of this experience is not always sufficiently shaped into art.

KELLER, KARL. "A Modern Version of Edward Taylor," *Early American Literature,* 9 (Winter 1975), 321–24. This critical note discusses Oates's imaginative use of Edward Taylor's poem in "Upon the Sweeping Flood."

KUEHL, LINDA, ed. "An Interview with Joyce Carol Oates," *Commonweal,* 91 (December 5, 1969), 307–10. Oates's responses to specific questions about own works, writing habits, and influence of other writers.

LISTON, WILLIAM T. "Her Brother's Keeper," *Southern Humanities Review,* 11 (Spring 1977), 195-203. Liston compares "In the Region of Ice" with a source in *Measure for Measure.*

MADDEN, DAVID. "The Violent World of Joyce Carol Oates," *The Poetic Image in 6 Genres.* Carbondale: Southern Illinois University Press, 1969, pp. 26–46. This appreciative essay-review of Oates's first four volumes characterizes her as the "second finest writer in America" (after Wright Morris) who sustains the intensity of her vision and credibility of characters and situations despite aesthetic flaws and "an apparent absence of art."

MARTIN, ALICE C. "Toward a Higher Consciousness: A Study of the Novels of Joyce Carol Oates," unpublished doctoral dissertation, Northern Illinois University, 1974. This study sees Oates's characters acting out "tragic rituals of sacrifice" in transformations of consciousness which demythologize the "myth of the isolated self."

McCONKEY, JAMES. "Joyce Carol Oates, *With Shuddering Fall,*" *Epoch,* 14 (Winter 1965), 185–88. This review article sees Shar and Karen as "extension of a society that has lost the sense of personal responsibility" and judges the violence "too shrill and too constant" and the two main characters not entirely convincing.

PARK, SUE S. "A Study in Counterpoint: Joyce Carol Oates's 'How I Contemplated the World from the Detroit House of Correction and Began My Life Over Again,'" *Modern Fiction Studies,* 22 (Summer

1976), 213–24. Park isolates the contrapuntal pattern of the story—
Bloomfield Hills/Detroit, mother/prostitute, father/junkie—which "is
ultimately traceable to the dichotomy within the girl herself."

PETITE, JOSEPH. "The Interrelatedness of Marriage, Passion and Female
Identity in the Fiction of Joyce Carol Oates," unpublished Ph.D.
dissertation, Kansas State University, 1976. Petite claims that Oates
dramatizes the negative effect of stereotyped roles on the personality
development of women.

———. " 'Out of the Machine': Joyce Carol Oates and the Liberation of
Woman," Kansas Quarterly, 9 (Spring 1977), 75-79. Of Oates's women,
Petite finds only Margo of "Dreams" and Nina of "Heavy Sorrow of the
Body" break out of the machine of femaleness.

PICKERING, SAMUEL F., JR. "The Short Stories of Joyce Carol Oates,"
Georgia Review, 28 (Summer 1974), 218–26. This broadly ranging essay
depicts Oates as representative of today's short-story writers whose
predominant weakness is a too-heavy emphasis on subjective,
psychological reality.

PINSKER, SANFORD. "Isaac Bashevis Singer and Joyce Carol Oates: Some
Versions of Gothic," Southern Review, 9 (Autumn 1973), 895–908.
This review article rather superficially and loosely compares Singer and
Oates as writers whose works have "gothic elements we feel."

———. "Suburban Molesters: Joyce Carol Oates' Expensive People,"
Midwest Quarterly, 19 (Autumn 1977), 89–103. Pinsker argues that the
novel is a parody of the reflexive mode and a study in comic nihilism.

ROCCO, CLAIRE JOYCE. "Flannery O'Connor and Joyce Carol Oates: Violence as Art," unpublished Ph.D. dissertation, University of Illinois,
1975. Rocco examines the "relationship between power and violence" in
the novels of the two writers and posits two major patterns of violence—
linguistic and personal.

STEVENS, CYNTHIA CHARLOTTE. "The Imprisoned Imagination: The Family in the Fiction of Joyce Carol Oates, 1960–1970," unpublished Ph.D.
dissertation, University of Illinois, 1974. Stevens argues that Oates's
imagination, dominated by Freudian patterns, creates fatalistic and
deterministic explanations for the motivation and action of her characters.

SULLIVAN, WALTER. "The Artificial Demon: Joyce Carol Oates and the
Dimension of the Real," Hollins Critic, December 1972, 1–12. This
review article finds Oates's best stories "among the very best being
written today" and the novels flawed, despite some convincing parts,
perhaps because there is a "problem of vision" in Oates's repeated
chronicling of violence as a prelude to insanity.

TAYLOR, GORDON O. "Joyce Carol Oates: Artist in Wonderland," Southern
Review, 10, i (1974), 490–503. Taylor outlines the general structure
of Wonderland, characterizes it as "inwardly spiraling, shell-like," and

suggests that the whole body of Oates's work can be seen as a similar "impulsive intensification."

"Transformations of Self: An Interview with Joyce Carol Oates," *Ohio Review*, 15, i (1973), 50–61. Extended, thoughtful responses by mail to interviewer's questions about her art.

UPHAUS, SUZANNE HENNING. "Boundaries: Both Physical and Metaphysical," *Canadian Review of American Studies*, 8 (Fall 1977), 236-42. A review article of *Crossing the Border* focusing on Oates's perceptions of Canada.

WALKER, CAROLYN. "Fear, Love, and Art in Oates's 'Plot,' " *Critique: Essays in Modern Fiction*, 15, i (1973), 59–70. Walker isolates Oates's frequent depiction of the Outsider and his attempt to impose a pattern and meaning on life through fictionalizing and closely analyzes the complex narration of "Plot."

WALLER, G. F. "Joyce Carol Oates' *Wonderland*: An Introduction," *Dalhousie Review*, 54 (Autumn 1974), 480–90. Waller finds *Wonderland* Oates's "most completely realized novel" and emphasizes its deterministic social context: the American idealistic Wonderland is really a materialistic wasteland which frustrates attempts to define the nature of individual personality.

WEGS, JOYCE M. "'Don't You Know Who I Am?': The Grotesque in Oates's 'Where Are You Going, Where Have You Been?,' " *Journal of Narrative Technique*, 5 (January 1975), 66–72. This close reading of the story perceptively argues that Oates's use of the grotesque adds to the multidimensional implications—especially to Arnold Friend's identity as the Arch Fiend, the devil-in-disguise.

———. "The Grotesque in Some American Novels of the Nineteen-Sixties: Ken Kesey, Joyce Carol Oates, Sylvia Plath," unpublished Ph.D. dissertation, University of Illinois, 1973. Wegs argues that Oates's work has an "ordered substructure" of images reflecting her sense of the "grotesque chaos of life."

2. Bibliography

CATRON, DOUGLAS M. "A Contribution to a Bibliography of Works by and about Joyce Carol Oates," *American Literature*, 49 (November 1977), 399–414. A supplement to McCormick's list which is also useful but incomplete (and misleading in the subsection entitled "Translations").

McCORMICK, LUCIENNE P. "A Bibliography of Works by and about Joyce Carol Oates," *American Literature*, 43 (March 1971), 124–32. A useful listing that is, however, incomplete and quite outdated.

Index

170